ROSS P. PADDOCK

APOSTOLIC ROOTS

AN INTERRACIAL HERITAGE

Second Edition

EDITOR-IN-CHIEF
Eric A. Beda

ALPHA OMEGA

Published in the United States by
Alpha Omega Publishing Company
P.O. Box 353, Jackson, MI 49204

Library of Congress Control Number: 2020941055

ISBN: 978-1-7320586-6-8

All Scripture quotations are derived from the Holy Bible, King James Version and New King James Version.

Alpha Omega Publishing Company publishes books that promote the discussion and understanding of the Pentecostal movement throughout the world since the Day of Pentecost. These books are made possible by the enthusiasm of our readers; the support of a committed group of donors, large and small; the collaboration of our many partners in the independent media and ecclesiastical organizations; booksellers, who often hand-sell Alpha Omega Publishing books; librarians; and above all by our authors.

Books may be purchased in quantity and/or special sales by contacting the publisher:

Alpha Omega Publishing
E: info@omegapublishing.org
www.omegapublishing.org

Printed in the United States of America

This book is dedicated to all those who love the truth and are committed to passing it down to the next generation.

The things that thou hast heard of me among many witnesses, the same commit thou to faithful men, who shall be able to teach others also (2 Tim 2:2).

APOSTLE PAUL

PREFACE

It has been more than a quarter of a century since Bishop Ross Perry Paddock's original edition of the book, *Apostolic Roots* was printed. Since it was first published, the book remained in print without revision. At last, our organization received permission to revise and rename the book in an attempt to provide more content around leaders that guided various Pentecostal organizations, and how those results impacted the Pentecostal movement in the United States from Charles Parham's Bible school to William Seymour's Azusa Street Mission. The new title, *Apostolic Roots: An Interracial Heritage*, was thoughtfully chosen and it reflects the current disposition of Pentecostal organizations in the U.S. I have edited and added the subtitle "An Interracial Heritage" in part to reflect the overshadowing impact of organizational changes during the 20th-century charismatic movement due to the disdained racial differences that have wedged Pentecostal organizations. The subtitle points to the willingness of the parent organization of all Pentecostal organizations, Pentecostal Assemblies of the World, Inc., to embrace racial diversity when it was unpopular for the dominant race and those of the minority race to be in fellowship. In the 19th and 20th century it was unpopular for blacks and whites to associate in a racially segregated era.

CONTENTS

APOSTOLIC ROOTS

INTERRACIAL HERITAGE

FOREWORD

This book examines the history of the Pentecostal movement in the U.S. through the 20th century, with special emphasis on the manner in which it has progressed from rejection by popular religious culture in its early days to acceptance. Pentecostal Apostolic pioneers such as Garfield Haywood, Morris Golder, Karl F. Smith, and Andrew David Urshan have shaped the history of the Apostolic era during the 20th century.

I have read many books in my lifetime, including the Holy Bible more than fifty times but have not read a more comprehensive firsthand account of the Pentecostal movement in the 20th century than in this book. Bishop Ross Paddock has done an impeccable job of sharing his account of the history of the Pentecostal Assemblies of the World and the various organizations that originated from its inception.

I was born in Portsmouth, Ohio, April 1, 1930, which was a transitional period for a number of Pentecostal groups. Growing up my father, John Andrew James was known as a serious person, an analytical thinker, and a devout Methodist pastor. But change came into our family when my mother, Bertha James, received the Gospel, and was baptized in the name of Jesus and filled with the precious Holy Ghost in 1931. I often say, my first birth made me a citizen of the United States of America, and the second birth gained me citizenship in heaven.

I am Apostolic from the crown of my head to the sole of my feet. I am Pentecostal in experience and Apostolic in doctrine. The Gospel is the world's greatest message and the Apostolic doctrine is the world's best practice by which the gospel is bestowed upon man. This book gives an account of men and women over the years that have committed to the preservation of this great Apostolic message. The compilation of this Apostolic history is necessary for the library of every Pentecostal believer.

Elder Johnny James
The Walking Bible

INTRODUCTION

It is needful for me to start with the Bible since it is the origin of Pentecostal Apostolic heritage also known as Pentecostal Oneness heritage. The first part of this volume will be a brief Bible prelude which will lead us into the history of the Pentecostal Oneness movement in the United States; specifically, in the area of the development of the Pentecostal Assemblies of the World.

What I attempted to emphasize in this book is the latter rain day and not about the early church that you may have read in your Bible. We have the history of the Acts of the Apostles, the twenty-one epistles, the four gospels, and the Book of Revelation. While it is good to know where we have come from, it is far more important today to know where we are going as this will be very helpful. The volume addresses the history of Pentecostal Oneness organizations from the beginning of the 20th century through 1978, and the growth of other Oneness organizations that sprung up from the Pentecostal Assemblies of the world. The volume covers the history of pastors, bishops, and other significant persons that have contributed to the Pentecostal Assemblies of the World.

The Christian Apologist, Dr. Alistair Edgar McGrath, noted that one of the most significant developments in the history of Christianity during the 20th century in the U.S. was the rise of the Pentecostal movement. Also known as the charismatic movement, the glossolalia or xenolalia experience affirms the power of the Holy Spirit as described in the New Testament, mainly in the Acts of the Apostles.[1] The 20th-century Pentecostal movement can be traced back to a Caucasian evangelist by the name of Charles Fox Parham (1873–1929). Sometime in 1901, he set out the basic ideas of what became the core of Pentecostalism. They included the belief of speaking in tongues and baptism of the Holy Spirit after the conversion of the believer. These ideas were later developed by William Joseph Seymour (1870–1922), an African American pastor, who presided over a major charismatic revival known as the Azusa Street Mission in Los Angeles, which lasted from 1906 to 1909. This marked the beginning of most major Pentecostal organizations in the United States of America and around the world, such as the Assemblies of God, Church of God in Christ, United Pentecostal Churches, Pentecostal Assemblies of the World, and others[2].

It was estimated the membership of Pentecostal movements has reached over 300 million people in over 230 countries by the end of the 1980s.[3] In recent years, it is calculated that there are at least 250 million confessed members worldwide and it is widely accepted that the Pentecostal faith is the most dynamic and fastest-growing sector of Christianity in the world today. It is likely to surpass other forms of Christianity in the 21st century. As a global religious movement, Pentecostal Christians have succeeded in reaching

---

[1] See Tyson (1992), for an insightful historical account of the Pentecostal movement.

[2] See Tyson (1992), for an insightful historical account of the Pentecostal movement.

[3] See "World Religions Religion Statistics Geography Church Statistics". Retrieved 5 March 2015

many cultures of the world, including reaching people across social and racial divisions in both urban and rural areas, and among both the middle classes and the poor.[4]

The Pentecostal teaching is couched in the creed that is only one race, the human race. All are equal when filled with the Holy Spirit and the Spirit has the ability to liberate both men and women. Particularly concerning the Pentecostal Apostolic faith. It was noted by the author that this faith is strongly egalitarian in its stance and that relationships were not based on class, race, gender, or ethnicity, but on the idea that all areas children of God. However, racial segregation pressure of the 19th and 20th centuries crept into churches and created denominational lines among Pentecostals.

---

[4] See Harvey (2000), how Pentecostals have transcended cultural and racial boundaries to connect people with the gospel.

$\sim 1 \sim$

KEEP YOURSELVES IN THE LOVE OF GOD

But ye, beloved, building up yourselves on your most holy faith, praying in the Holy Ghost, keep yourselves in the love of God, looking for the mercy of our Lord Jesus Christ unto eternal life (Jude 1:20-21).

THE LOVE OF GOD

Now, the subject of these two verses is found in the first line of Verse 21, *Keep yourselves in the love of God*; the second line continues by saying *looking for the mercy of our Lord Jesus Christ unto eternal life*. That's what we're looking for us to keep ourselves in the love of God that we might obtain that eternal life.

How do we, *keep ourselves in the love of God?* Two things we ought to do, and they are found in verse 20, by *building up yourselves in your most holy faith* and by *praying in the Holy Ghost*. I am not going to deal with prayer as I feel you know what it means to pray in the Holy Ghost. The Bible says, *we should pray with all prayer and supplication in the spirit* (Ephesians 6:18). This means that any prayer that is said in the flesh is not going to even go pass the level of our head except if it is prayed in the spirit. Simply put, we pray in the Holy Ghost. Building ourselves in our most holy faith is going to be our subject. But now these two things that we are to do are for the purpose *to keep ourselves in the love of God*. Just to keep the record straight, we will have to understand what the Bible means by *keeping ourselves in the love God*.

Preachers would typically state that God loves everybody. On the contrary, the Bible says[God] *hates the hypocrite and He is angry with the wicked every day* (Psalms 7:11).What we have to realize is, *God so loved the world that he gave his only begotten son, and whosoever believeth in him, should not perish but have everlasting life* (John 3:16). It was the world that God loved, not every individual in the world-and he loved the world to the extent that He sent His son, that *whosoever believeth in him should not perish, but have everlasting life*. Who then, was it that God loved? Is it the individuals in the world or is it those who would believe in His son? I know this may come as kind of a blow to some, but I will explain it to you as we go along.

There is a parable that I would like for you to ponder. The parable states: *The kingdom of heaven is like unto treasure that was hidden in a field which when the man hath found for joy thereof, he sold all that he had and purchased the field* (Matthew 13:44). You ought to know that the man who sold all he had and bought the field was the Lord Jesus Christ. Also, the treasure that was hidden in the field was the Church, and the field is the world. Why did He buy the world? Did He want to become a farmer? Most certainly not the reason He bought the world is to get the treasure that was in the world. So, what was it that He loved – the world or the treasure? It was the treasure. And so, when Jesus went to Calvary's cross to pay the price for the salvation of every man, woman, and child who has ever lived or ever will live, He did not expect to get everyone. He expected only to get that particular treasure of which we are. *They shall be mine when I make up my jewels saith, the Lord* (Malachi 3:17). So, God loved the world that much and that love is extended to everyone.

There is another scripture to note: *Behold what matter of love the father hath bestowed upon us, that we shall be called the sons of God. Therefore, the world knoweth us not because it knew him not* (1 John 3:1).The manner of love that God bestowed upon us was the love that made us sons of God and this is the love that is upon the Church, which is not upon the world. The world knows nothing about it but God hath bestowed that love on us.

Now, you understand that love because you are the children of God. I am assuming that you who are reading at this time have the born-again experience. Meaning, you have heard the gospel of truth, you have believed it, you have repented, you have been baptized in the name of Jesus Christ for the remission of your sins, you are filled with the Holy Ghost per the Bible's evidence of *speaking in other tongues as the spirit of God gives utterance (Acts 2:4)*, and you are now going on to perfection. These are the ones whom the love of God has been bestowed upon. The world is not in that love that we are in, but if we are going to inherit the benefits by being in it we have to keep ourselves in it. It doesn't make any difference that you have started. The question is, are you going to make it to the end of the race? Are you going to be ready to go when Jesus calls for His church? When He comes, he's coming for those who are ready, not those who are getting ready. So, to keep yourself in it, you have to keep yourself ready to answer the call.

How do we *keep ourselves in the love of God?* I will illustrate. When I was a little boy, we had our little boy's clubs, our playhouses (no girls allowed). And we thought that God surely made a great mistake when He created the female gender. We thought this world would be a wonderful place if there weren't any girls (we were just being boys, you know). But things began to change as we developed, and suddenly our eyes began to open, and we saw a difference in those girls. The next thing you know, we began to believe that girls were the most glorious creatures that God has ever created, and we just loved all of them.

I will use myself as an example here. I was in love with every girl I saw, I fell in love--or so it seemed. I was engaged five times before I met my wife, and we were still children when we were married. I'll tell you, anybody at the age of 17 years is too young for marriage. I know because we were both just seventeen when we were married. I continued to grow for four years after I was married. By the time one would say I was old enough to be married we already had three children in the family. What I'm trying to say to you is, I was just in love with every girl I saw. However, a day came when I had to make a choice, and in the ceremony, there was a remark that goes like this: "Forsaking all others, I'll keep myself unto thee as long as we both shall live." But, my true vow was, "of all the women in this world, no matter how beautiful, gracious, kind, loving, and generous-hearted they might be, I'm turning my back on every one of them and I am choosing you, and I will be faithful to you, and you alone, as long as we both shall live." These vows were taken 55 years ago and I'm still keeping them. What am I saying? Although I loved all the girls for some time, a time came when I set my love on one particular one. On a much larger scale, God so loved the world until the time came, that He set His love on one particular one, and that's a chaste virgin, the espoused virgin, the bride of Christ, the Lamb's wife, the Mother of all, the Church. So, if you tell me that God so loved the world, I'll agree with you. But, I'll respond by saying, he set his love on one, and that one is the Church. This is the love of God in the world today and we are to keep ourselves in the love of God. Please, don't try to tell me that God loves everything that's going on in this world, and I can't be very sure that He loves everything that's going on in the church, because there are some things in which we haven't reached perfection yet.

So, the subject before us is, *keep yourselves in the love of God* (Jude1:20-21). That is, if you are in the church then stay in it. Stay in the church in such a manner that God's love can be extended to you constantly, and when He comes for His church, you will be included in that number. This is what Jude is talking about.

~ 2 ~

YOUR MOST HOLY FAITH: HOLINESS

But ye, beloved, building up yourselves on your most holy faith, praying in the Holy Ghost (Jude 1:20).

MOST HOLY FAITH

How are we to do this? By doing two things, and we have already passed by the prayer. *Building up yourselves in your most holy faith.* What is your most holy faith? One of the uses of a comma in a sentence is to prevent repetition. So, as I quote to you from Hebrews (12:14), *Follow peace with all men and holiness,* comma, *without which no man shall see the Lord.* Now, let me leave out the comma and put in the repetition that the comma avoided. *Follow peace with all men and holiness with all men, without which no man shall see the Lord.* So, you thought holiness only relates to your relationship with God? Oh, no! Holiness relates to your relationship with me and all other brothers and sisters. And I can assure you that if you have that kind of life, you will never have to worry about being a gay, or a lesbian, or a fornicator, or an adulterer because your holiness is going to be shown in your relationship with your fellow man. We are to build up ourselves in our most holy faith so we must recognize, then, that our faith will bring about holiness in our relationship with man and God.

The First Commandment says, *Hear O Israel, the Lord your God is one Lord, and thou shall love the Lord thy God with all your heart, with all your mind, with all your soul, with all your strength* (Deuteronomy 6:4-5). And the second goes like this: *thou shalt love thy neighbor as thyself* (Matthew 22:39). So immediately you say that's number one, that's the first one and the most important, and number two will follow along as the second. But I'm going to reverse the order and say this: If you don't keep number two you will never be able to keep number one. For how can you love God whom you have not seen if you can't love your brother whom you have seen? If you can't love me, don't tell me you love God. If you don't love your brothers and sisters, no matter their nationality, economic status, ethnicity, or academic achievement then there is no way in the world you can love God.

The international evangelist, Billy Graham said, "racial and ethnic hostility is the foremost social problem facing our world today. From the systematic horror of 'ethnic cleansing' in Bosnia to the random violence ravaging our inner cities, our world seems caught up in a tidal wave of racial and ethnic tension. The hostility threatens the very foundation of modern society"[5] so, it comes right back to this: it's our relationship with each other; "to build up ourselves on our most holy faith" (Jude 1:20). And the faith that we have in God should bring about holiness with one another. You can never show the world the righteousness of God in a segregated church or in any manner of segregation. It doesn't make any difference how it's segregated. It has to be a church consisting with various kinds of people. It is imperative that the church wakes up, discern the signs of the times and recognize that we must relate differently to people who are unlike us if we are going to go up together with the Lord. Scripture says, *there is neither Jew nor Greek, there is neither bond nor free, there is neither male nor female: for ye are all one in Christ Jesus* (Galatians 3:28). The righteousness of God causes human diversity to flourish. We have to remember that it is wrong to segregate, separate, or look down on anybody for any reason. The righteousness of God will never be shown to the world in a segregated church. The apostle Paul said, *I am not ashamed of the gospel of Christ for it is the power of God unto salvation to everyone who believeth to the Jew first, and also to the Greek* (Romans 1:16). But he did not stop there; he wrote in the seventeenth

---

[5] See Harvey (2000), how Pentecostals have transcended cultural and racial boundaries to connect people with the gospel.

verse: "for therein" [in the gospel, bringing the Jew and the Greek together] is the righteousness of God revealed.

Today, the gospel assembles all races: the black, white, red, brown, and yellow together into one body, thereby, making us love each other as brethren; this is the righteousness of God revealed from faith to faith. Christians will never show the world the righteousness of God until they can get to the place where we allow our faith to make us colorblind, ignoring nationality differences as well as economic status. Our unity and reconciliatory efforts could be the greatest witness of the church in these last days. Paul criticized the Corinthian Church because of division among members. On this occasion, the source of their division was related to economic status. For when they came together to have communion at the local church, those who had financial means brought their dinner with them whereas those of low socioeconomic status could not afford to bring anything to eat. The brother who brought his steak dinner with his wine ate and drank until he became drunk before taking communion whereas his poor neighbor sat in his presence in starvation. Apparently, the wealthy individual had no concern for his starving neighbor. Paul said when you eat unworthily you bring damnation or condemnation onto your soul. And why was there unworthiness? They didn't recognize it was the body of Christ. What is the body of Christ? The body of Christ is not referring to the physical body of Christ, but it's referring to the spiritual body of Christ-the Church of the living God. The wealthy Christians did not recognize the need of their brethren or they disregarded the need of their brethren. So, you see how easy it is to get off on the wrong foot? I just have to let you know that we have to recognize and love one another, and this is what the holy faith will do for us if we build up ourselves in our most holy faith.

~ 3 ~

HOW MANY FAITHS ARE THERE?

One Lord, one faith, and one baptism. One God and Father of all, who is above all, and through all, and in you all (Ephesians 4:5).

ONE LORD, ONE FAITH, AND ONE BAPTISM

Now having established that it is holiness we need in all of our relationships with another, we now ask, "What is our faith?" Well, first of all our faith is what we believe. How many faiths are there? Speaking from the scriptures, *there's one body and one spirit even as ye are called in one hope of your calling. One Lord, one faith, and one baptism. One God and Father of all, who is above all, and through all, and in you all* (Ephesians 4:5). There are more than four thousand faiths in this world, but there is only one which God recognizes. How many churches are there? There are many churches, more than a thousand. But God recognizes just one. Jesus said unto his disciples, *on this rock I build my church* (Matthew 16:18). He is saying that right in the midst of all the churches that men are building, "I'm going to build mine." The church that Jesus intended to build is known as the body of Christ today. It's what we believe with all our hearts as the true church of the living God.

We have *"the"* faith, not *"a"* faith, so we are to build ourselves in the most holy faith. In Jude verse 3, *Beloved, when I gave all diligence to write unto you of the common salvation.* Speaking of "the common salvation", there are different uses of the word common. For example, the expression "a common woman" will immediately make you think about a woman who will give herself to any man who comes along. But in this manner the scripture has a different meaning to the term. The common faith means this: to everybody that has it, it is the same faith; it is common to everyone who has it. So there are not different faiths but only one faith, and one salvation, the common salvation. Any other faith you have other than the aforementioned, is not faith. One may call it such but it is not faith. *It was needful for me to write unto you, and exhort you that ye should earnestly contend for the faith which was once delivered unto the saints* (Jude 1:3). Note: "It was needful" can mean it was necessary. *What* made it necessary? This was revealed in verse 4: *For there are certain men crept in unawareness, who were before of old ordained to this condemnation, ungodly men, turning the grace of our God into lasciviousness, and denying the only Lord God, and our Lord Jesus Christ* (Jude 1:4).Saint Jude encouraged those that have the aforementioned faith, to contend for it unless certain ungodly persons corrupt the faith and cause many to denied the only Lord God, who is the Lord Jesus Christ.

~ 4 ~

WHAT DO YOU SEE?

Beloved, when I gave all diligence to write unto you of the common salvation, it was needful for me to write unto you, and exhort you that ye should earnestly contend for the faith which was once delivered unto the saints. For there are certain men crept in unawares, who were before of old ordained to this condemnation, ungodly men, turning the grace of our God into lasciviousness, and denying the only Lord God, and our Lord Jesus Christ (Jude 1:3-4).

CERTAIN MEN CREPT IN UNAWARES

Many Christians see predestination in these verses. and they feel that an individual is predestinated either to be lost or to be saved. However, this is not true as these individuals were not predestined to condemnation. The doctrine of predestination is a central part of Unconditional Eternal Security and is associated with the sovereignty of God. The doctrine of Unconditional Eternal Security has been around from the time of John Calvin, who receives the credit for propagating this erroneous teaching[6]. The fact that we can be eternally saved in Christ is not the issue, but to espouse the teaching that "once in Christ and never out" is a doctrine that is not supported by the apostles' doctrine. *Now unto him that is able to keep you from falling, and to present you faultless before the presence of his glory with exceeding joy, to the only wise God our Savior* (Jude 1:24-25). See 2 Timothy 1:12 as well. We are assured by these and other references that God's power, through the Holy Ghost, is sufficient to sustain the saints in every situation and there is no justification to fail, at least on God's part. Essentially, the ideology imposes on believers that God predetermines before an individual is born whether he or she will be saved. If one is predestined by God's sovereignty to go astray, eternally damned, then there is no way to redeem the individual. On the contrary, if one is predestined to be saved by God's choice, then there is no way the person can be eternally damned. The doctrine describes that people have no control or choice over their eternal destiny and God will save them at the very end even though they may sin to their last breath. This premise is false and the scriptural references are ample evidence of the error in this philosophy. There are only two predestined entities in the Bible, entities determined to be

---

[6] See Steele and Thomas (1963)

and no possibility of change. Persons are not predestined with the exception of Jesus Christ, the Son of God.

His coming was predetermined in God's plan of salvation before the foundation of the world and could not be altered from God's original purpose.

We are redeemed by *the precious blood of Christ as of a lamb without blemish and without spot, who was fore ordained before the foundation of the world* and *whose names are not written in the Book of Life of the lamb slain from the foundation of the world* (1 Peter 1:19-20; Revelation 13:8). The second is the church, *"according as he has chosen us (the church) in him before the foundation of the world, that we should be Holy and without blame before him in love"* (Ephesians 1: 4). The church, also known as the body of Christ, is predestined to Heaven and not the individuals who make up the church.

One of the best examples that I have heard about predestination: a planet hat is scheduled to depart from New York at 10 AM will arrive in South Africa 17 hours later. As a ticket holder, if I miss the opportunity to board that flight, regardless the plane will arrive at its predetermined destination. The plane is predestine for South Africa regardless if I missed my flight or if I was on board. As a Christian, if I am not in good standing with God then I will miss the opportunity to be part of his plan and will not arrive at the predetermined destination of the church.

God knows who will be saved and who will not because of his fore knowledge. He is the omniscient God. However, this fore knowledge does not compel an individual to believe nor does it cause hindrance in one's faith. Faith in the Word of God is left to the individual's choice (Luke 10:20). God's fore knowledge offers him access to fore see the beginning and end of matters before they happen and is privy to our thoughts "afar off'" (Psalm 139:1-4). *The Lord is a God of knowledge, and by him actions (motives) are weighed* (1 Samuel 2:3).

It isn't that God doesn't know who is going to be saved. He knows whether I am going to make it or not. Obviously, I'm trying my best to make the journey and I am fully determined to make it, but maybe I won't. Apostle Paul said, *for I keep under my body and bring it into subjection lest after having preached the gospel to others, I myself should become a castaway* (1 Corinthians 9:27). If the great apostle to the Gentiles expressed the fact that it was possible for him to forfeit his place in the kingdom of heaven as Judas forfeited his through transgression (Acts 1:25), then it's certainly possible for me to become a castaway as well. Fore knowledge offers God a foresight concerning what is forthcoming in the future. God knows what is going to occur in my future, but I don't. Scripture says that I should give the diligence to make my calling and election sure. He knows whether I'm going to make it or not. So, predestination is determined by the fore knowledge of God.

The Bible says, *Yea, and all that live Godly in Christ Jesus shall suffer persecution* (2 Timothy 3:12). How much persecution are we suffering as Christians in the United States these days? There has never been widespread persecution of Christians, per se. The worst thing that happens nowadays is people calling us names. You no longer suffer from a certain genre of persecution due to the laws of the land. In my experience, I have been beaten, choked, had my clothes torn off my back. Further, I have had buckets of ice water poured on me, my clothes covered with oil, and my shoes filled with oil. I had to work barefooted on a cement floor for eight hours one night while I was doing my job and my co-workers would come up behind me and spit tobacco juice at my feet in an attempt to make me angry. Also, I was burnt with hot irons and much more, all for the gospel of

Jesus Christ. Times have changed because you don't hear about such things happening anymore in the United States. As one exegesis of the text, the apostle Paul said all that lived Godly in Christ Jesus shall suffer persecution, but evil men and seducers shall act worse, deceiving and being deceived (2Timothy 3:12-13). So, what is the order of the day? It's not persecution, but deception. Evil men and seducers will get worse, deceiving and being deceived.

Deception is simply when a man is deceived, but he thinks he's right, and because he thinks he's right he makes it his duty to make everybody else believes what he now believes. So, what does he become? He was deceived and now he has become a deceiver. The worst problem we have to face today is false doctrine. Saint Jude spoke of false doctrine when it started in his time. He said, *Certain men have crept in already* (Jude 1:4). John also spoke of it that the *antichrist shall come* (1 John 2:18). Already there are many antichrists in the world. If it began back then, more than nineteen hundred years ago, then it must be worst today. False doctrine and not persecution is the device for Christians to be watchful of these today.

As I continue to exegesis Jude 1:3, *it was needful for me to write unto you.* The reason Jude wrote this was because of the proliferation of false doctrine during his time. He started out by saying, *when I give all diligence to write unto you...*If I can offer a parable for the moment on the text, *when I give all diligence to write.* I've written a few other books in the past. For seven years I have written an article every month in the Pentecostal Assemblies of the World's periodical, *Christian Outlook* with the exception of two months. When I initially complete an article I revise it paragraph by paragraph, correcting where necessary, to make certain I have said what I intended to say. After I am satisfied with that, I go back over what I have done and make additional corrections if there are any needed. I will continue this process until my article is completed to my satisfaction. Ultimately, when it is complete, and I am certain I said what I wanted to say. I then lay it down and let it get cold. Sometime later, I'll pick it up and read it again to make further corrections. When I am completely satisfied with all the handwritten edits, I then type the final draft. While I am typing I will further edit as I go along. Finally, when that document leaves my desk I feel confident that the final version is a reflection of what the Holy Spirit inspired me to pen.

I hope you can understand now when Jude said *when I gave all diligence to write unto you* (Jude 1:3). Essentially, he is saying, I didn't just sit down and draft my epistle in a hurry. What I have written may not be a long script but, the writing was thoughtful and diligently scripted to warn my brothers and sisters in Christ about the proliferation of false doctrine as I was inspired by the Holy Spirit.

What is the subject of the Book of Jude? He said that we should *earnestly contend for the faith once delivered to the saints* (Jude 1:3). May I add a little bit to this? Not to change it but to clarify it. You should earnestly contend for the faith that was once and for all delivered unto the saints. The faith is never to be published in any manner other than how which it was given, once, for all. The faith that was once delivered to the saints is the only faith we have any right to preach or teach today. We cannot preach our opinions or our own ideas, but we are to preach *the faith that was once delivered to the saints*. How was it delivered? It was delivered by the apostles. *How shall we escape if we neglect so great salvation, which at the first began to be spoken by the Lord, and afterwards was confirmed unto us by them that heard it, the Lord also bearing them witness by signs and wonders and diverse gifts of the Holy Ghost according to his own will* (Hebrews 2:3-4). The Book of Ecclesiastes states, a threefold cord is hard to break (4:12). You take a cord string and you may wrap it around your fingers, jerk it, and break it, but you take a double string and it will take double the strength. But if you take one that is a threefold cord and braid it, or twist it up together and pull, it is very unlikely to be easily broken.

~ 5 ~

THREEFOLD CORD OF GOD'S WORD

How shall we escape if we neglect so great salvation, which at the first began to be spoken by the Lord, and afterwards was confirmed unto us by them that heard it, the Lord also bearing them witness by signs and wonders and diverse gifts of the Holy Ghost according to his own will (Hebrews 2:3-4).

SIGNS AND WONDERS AND DIVERSE GIFTS

The threefold cord: the first, it first began to be spoken by the Lord; the second, the apostles came along and what did they say? The spoken word of the Lord Jesus was confirmed to them that heard it, they confirmed what Jesus had said. The apostles did not say anything contrary to what Jesus said, but what they said was a confirmation of what he had said. Now, what's the third cord? *The Lord also bore them witness by signs and wonders and diverse gifts of the Holy Ghost according to his own will* (Hebrews 2:4). The miracles that were wrought by the apostles were simply the Lord Jesus Christ bearing witness to the fact that what they said was a confirmation of what He had said. Do you see how simple it is? The Bible is so simple when you get it straight. But when you don't have it straight, it becomes full of confusion on occasions.

Jesus began to speak it, and then the apostles came along to reaffirm His words. Now, we do not have only Matthew, Mark, Luke, and John, but also Acts, and all the 21 Epistles, and the Book of Revelation as well, making 29 Books of the New Testament and all of this is the faith that was once delivered to the saints, so there isn't any use to concoct any new philosophy for the development of our Christian faith. What should we teach? All we have is what the apostles delivered to the church and what we should teach is the *Apostolic Roots*. Which is rooted in the apostolic doctrine and it's a great interracial heritage. How great is it? It is the only heritage you can have that will get you into God's heaven. I say that without any qualms. Absolutely nothing less than this will get you into God's heaven.

There is a common belief among some white Americans that we do not have racial problems in our churches. They'd like to think all of it has been resolved once people become the recipient of salvation whereas most folks of color feel there are on-going racial issues in our churches which explain the organizational divisions (e.g., Pentecostal of Assemblies of the Word versus United Pentecostal Churches, Church of God in Christ versus Assemblies of God, etc.). The call for reconciliation and unity in church organizations could be one of the greatest witnesses of the church to the world. Church leaders cannot be concerned about building their own kingdom but God's kingdom. The issue of racial division in church organizations must be confronted only through the power of the Holy Ghost. The issue is rooted in pride, fear, racial hatred, and division. If the church is going to be the example that the world will learn from, then it has to be through the power of the Holy Spirit, *Not by might, nor by power, but by my spirit* (Zechariah 4:6).

If we want to be ushered into God's heaven then we must forfeit our natural heritage and get a hold on God's heritage. It was first spoken by Jesus, *He that loveth father or mother more than me is not worthy of me: and he that loveth son or daughter more than me is not worthy of me* (Mathew 10:37). He spoke to the apostles about not identifying with family, ethnic heritage, or culture. Later, the apostle Paul reaffirms it by saying, *there is neither Jew nor Greek, there is neither bond nor free, there is neither male nor female: for ye are all one in Christ Jesus* (Galatians 3:28). Let us not be carried away by our pedigree and cultural identities, rather, let us be reconciled unto God. Our identities with family pedigree, ethnic heritage, or culture are not to be factors if we want to be part of God's family heritage and our identity with Christ becomes more important than self-identity. The church must reaffirm and teach the message we have inherited from the apostles. This is the threefold core of God's word.

What we must have is the faith that was once delivered to the saints, the Apostolic teachings from the beginning. We've got to earnestly strive, contend, argue, and fight for the faith that was once delivered to the saints. Why do we have to fight against those that will come up with false doctrines? Paul said in the Book of Acts, *after my departure shall grievous wolves enter in among you, not sparing the flock* (Acts 20:29). For what they come for is to destroy the sheep. This isn't talking about Christians, but people from outside of the body of Christ. These individuals will come in to attempt to influence the church. It's bad when they come in to destroy the flock, but pastors, as the under shepherds, have to protect God's people from them. It's bad, but do you know anything worse than this? I do. The next verse said, a*nd also of your own selves shall men arise, speaking perverse things, to draw away disciples after themselves* (Acts 20:30). There will be some in the midst of God's church that will teach contrary to the doctrine of the apostles to draw followers to themselves.

Now therefore ye men are no more strangers and foreigners, but fellow citizens with the saints, and of the household of God (Ephesians 2:19). We are now members of the household of God. *And are built upon the foundation of the apostles and prophets, Jesus Christ himself* (Ephesians 2:20). What is the foundation on which we are to build ourselves? The foundation of the apostles, and the prophets with Jesus Christ Himself being the chief cornerstone; and what did they preach? Jesus Christ, a confirmation of what He said and what He had already preached to them, not the imagination of their hearts. We are built upon the apostle's doctrine. So, where do we get our Apostolic roots? Let's go back to our origins now and see where we began, examining how we got to where we are today and where we've got to stay if we expect to go with Jesus when He returns.

Now Jesus Christ Himself is the chief cornerstone. When the word of God is rightly divided, it fits together, but when it's not rightly divided there is confusion and contradiction. When we are fitly framed together, we're one body in Christ. *In whom all the building fitly framed together groweth unto a holy temple in the Lord* (Ephesians 2:21). Notice, this is the writing of Paul, a Jewish bishop writing to the Gentile churches in Ephesus. And in the first verse he said, *and you hath he quickened who were dead in trespasses and sin* (Ephesians 2:1). Then the second verse, he lays them low and he tells them what they were. I suspect some of them at first, may have easily been offended and say, "what business do you have talking to us Gentiles like that?" And I guess they might have had a point, but he didn't stop there. He continued in the third verse, *among whom also we [Jews] had our conversation in times past in the lusts of our flesh and we're children of wrath, even as others* (Ephesians 2:3). What he's saying is that you Gentiles were morally corrupt, but we Jews were just as bad. Further, God, *who is rich in mercy, for his great love, loved us even when we were dead in our sins, hath quickened us together.*

In verses 2 and 3, Paul clearly shared that both Jews and Gentiles were altogether in sin. So, there was togetherness in our sinful state. Isn't the world together today? If you don't believe it, read what John said, we know the whole world lies in wickedness. But now, he hath giving life to both groups together and not separately, and hath raised them up together. If we are raised up in Christ, we have been raised up together. The day is long gone when we fight one another. The time for us now is to get together because *He hath raised us up together [quickened us together]* and made us sit together in heavenly places. Christ rose first and we shall soon follow. We're going to be all caught up together to meet the Lord in the air and the Lord is going to make all saints live together throughout all of eternity (1 Thessaloni-

33

ans 4 and 5). Hence, if you can't get along together on earth, then don't expect to go up to heaven. Who's going up to heaven? The individuals that have learned how to live in unity in God's church on earth. It is time for the saints to stop fighting one another and get together, recognizing *only that as we work together to this whole building fitly framed together, and grow to a holy temple of the Lord. In whom ye also are built for a habitation of God through the Spirit* (Ephesians 2:21-22).

Once upon a time, a major problem arose in one of our churches in Michigan. Typically, when there is a major issue in a diocese, the respective diocesan was invited to judge the case. There was a sister that said, "I've been saved a long time ago so I know what holiness is" and she was just laying out about how everyone else was wrong except her. I said, "my sister, you might have known what holiness was and if you did, you ought to know what you're doing now is far from holiness." We may as well recognize the fact that we have to live together and cannot fight one another, and still make it to heaven. We must have what was given to us in the days of the apostles and every one of us who is going to make it to heaven must have it; nothing less than this will do. If we know the truth and don't show it, then we're responsible for that knowledge and will be judged accordingly. Some people don't know the truth and will not be judged for what they don't know. But the ones who know shall be judged accordingly. And what is the body of Christ? It's a building of people that are fitly framed together who are growing together. The body of Christ should not be pulling apart, but growing together. Friend, don't tell me you have the Holy Ghost and you are fighting one another. I would answer back and say, you may have *had* the Holy Ghost but you don't have Him now because He doesn't act that way.

Be patient therefore, brethren, unto the coming of the Lord. Behold, the husbandman waiteth for the precious fruit of the earth (James 5:7). What is that precious fruit of the earth? It's the Church, the saints, and not only those who are in now, but those who will get in between now and that time. When that time will be, no man knows. But until Jesus comes, we are to be patient and wait, because the Lord is waiting for the precious fruit of the earth. *And hath long patience for it, until he receives the early and latter rain.* Who then is going to make up this precious fruit of the earth or His jewels as we said at another standpoint? Those that came in the Early Rain and those who will come in the Latter Rain; there is a period of more than a thousand years between the former and the latter rain, according to Bible scholars.

The early and latter rain is referring to the outpouring of the Holy Spirit between two periods. Specifically, the early rain is referring to the beginning of the outpouring of the Holy Ghost during the day of Pentecost following the ascension of Jesus Christ and the latter rain is referring to the inundation of the Holy Ghost in our current time. In recent years, it is reckoned that there are at least 250 million adherents globally and it the most dynamic and fastest-growing sector of Christianity in the world today; it is likely to surpass other forms of Christianity in the 21st century.[7] During the farm season in biblical times, there was the former rain followed by the planting season, afterward the crops began to grow and had taken roots, and then came the dry season. After the dry season there was the latter rain, and then came the ripening of the crops before the harvest. The outpouring of the Holy Ghost in the church transpired in a period that

---

[7] See Synan's (2001) work on the outpouring of the Holy Spirit in the Twentieth Century.

can be illustrated as the dry season between the former and the latter rain.

Be glad then, ye children of Zion, [that was Israel] and rejoice in the Lord your God; for he hath given you the former rain moderately, and he will cause to come down for you the rain, the former rain, and the latter rain in the first month (Joel 2:23). God gave the nation of Israel the former rain and he gave the current church age the latter rain. The former rain was giving moderately at the beginning and the world was not as populated as it is today. The Church is universal, but that portion of the world that was known during that time was just a little portion that surrounded the Mediterranean Sea. But today, the outpouring of the Holy Ghost is in greater abundance than it was back then. Originally, the opportunity of the Holy Spirit rain was intended for Israel, but we are the recipients of this experience because Israel turned their backs on Jesus and rejected Him. So, the Lord opened the door to the Gentiles and allowed us to come in for a period of time. But look out because Israel will be brought back into favor with God in the tribulation period but we (Gentiles) will have no second chance.

The apostle Peter derived his sermon from the Book of Joel (2:28-29). Peter said, *these men are not drunk, as you think....* This is new wine from heaven. He stood up out of the eleven apostles and said,

ye men of Judea, and all ye that dwell at Jerusalem, be this known unto you, and hearken unto my words....These men are not drunk as you suppose seeing it is but the third hour of the day. But this is that, which was spoken by the prophet Joel; and it shall come to pass on the last days saith God that I will pour out of my spirit upon all flesh. And your sons and your daughters shall prophesy and your young men shall see visions and your old men shall dream dreams: And on my servants, and on my hand maidens I will pour out in those days of my spirit, and they shall prophesy (Acts 2:14-18).

It is illustrated through these verses that the outpouring of the Holy Spirit was not limited to a specific gender of human, but it was intended to include both male and female, the young and the aged. It shows God has always had a great purpose for the diversity among his people. This purpose is to fill the earth with God's glory and requires that humanity in all of its diversity reflect the image of God in the earth (McNeil and Richardson, 2004). Some Christians have embraced the Great Commission--the call to preach the gospel to everyone; whereas others have embraced the Great Commandment, preaching the importance of loving our neighbors as ourselves, and to see all as fellow citizens of heaven. Neither the Great Commandment nor the Great Commission should be preferred one over the other but the need to proclaim both simultaneously will spread the godly influence that the Lord desires to see among his people.

Incidentally, if anybody does not believe that women should be preachers then the individual should revisit the historical event of the day of Pentecost to find not just men, but women were included in God's plan. I want you to know that back in the Book of Joel, he said, "it shall come to pass after...." The first pouring out of the Early Rain, and after it, came the Latter Rain, and that's where we are today-the Latter Rain.

~ 6 ~

START OF THE LATTER RAIN CHURCH

Ask ye of the Lord rain in the time of the latter rain; so the Lord shall make bright clouds, and give them showers of rain, in every one grass in the field (Zechariah 10:1).

GIVE THEM SHOWERS

When the apostles were martyred and John was the last one standing (Foxe, 2009), and this was before the end of the first century. The apostle John died around 100 A.D. of natural death according to various sources (Thomas, 2016). The church was approximately 70 years old when the last of the apostles passed on. It was not long after that various false doctrines began to take over after the defenders (fathers) of the faith fell asleep in Christ. There were various Christian organizations and concepts that came on the scene including Catholicism and the Nicene Creed. The Catholic Churches posed that Peter was their first pope; don't believe it. Peter died before the turn of the century but the Catholic Church was not founded until 150 A.D. How could Peter, who had been dead for more than 50 years, be the first pope of the organization? Later, the Council of Nicaea under Constantine the Great introduced the doctrine of the Trinity which was ultimately adopted by many Christian organizations.

The concept of Trinity or God in three persons (Father, Son, and Holy Ghost) has become an embedded tradition in nearly every Christian doctrine. Its inception dates back around the third century after the day of Pentecost. History in forms us the Council of Nicaea essentially introduced the Nicene Creed in 325 A.D. However, the Council of Constantinople made inroads for "the doctrine which the Council of Nicaea had left imperfect of three persons in one God" (Bellitto, 2002).

We, the three Emperors, will that our subjects follow the religion taught by St. Peter to the Romans, professed by those saintly prelates, Damascus, Pontiff of Rome, and Peter, Bishop of Alexandria, that they believe the one divinity of the Father, Son, and the Holy Spirit, of majesty co-equal in the Holy Trinity. We will that those who embrace this creed be called Catholic Christians. We brand all the senseless followers of other religions by the infamous name of heretics and forbid their conventicles to assume the name of Churches. The decree was endorsed and solidified in the names of Gratian, Valentinian II, and Theodosius. This was the birth of the doctrine of Trinity; as said by Dean Milman in his writing of the History of Christianity, 'the religion of the whole Roman world was enacted by two feeble boys and a rude Spanish soldier' (Schaff, 1882). Since that time, the overwhelming majority of men's eyes have been darkened and they have not been able to come to the truth (Stannus, 1883).

The first churches that were founded by the apostles went into total darkness and lost the knowledge of the oneness of God in Jesus Christ. The lost church believes the Father, the Son, and the Holy Ghost as three distinct persons. Those that espouse to the Trinitarian doctrine expects to see three persons on God's throne in spite of the Bible indicating there's only one. For centuries, the Catholic Church has tremendously influenced the Christian church to its way of thinking. There is a scriptural verse that says: *God never left himself without a witness* (Acts 14:17). In my experience, many preachers have misinterpreted the text for something Scripture has not intended. Scripture says God never left Himself without a witness meaning, he did good and gave them rain, seasons, and crops to grow, but I firmly believe that there's never been a time that God hasn't had somebody,

41

somewhere that was filled with His spirit. Until the time the reformers came along starting with Martin Luther. Martin Luther never intended to come out of the Catholic Church, but his intent was to correct the error and abuse of the Catholic organization. In his attempt to correct the various types of abuses he was forced out of the Catholic Church. Naturally, those who followed him drew together and formed what we know today as the Lutheran Church. Now, many of those followers were martyred because they turned away from the Catholic Church, and even Martin Luther himself was martyred in 1546--more than 400 years ago[8].

If you read carefully in the Book of Joel (1:4), he tells you about how it was going to happen. He said there would be the Palmerworm and the caterpillar, etc. They would gradually devour and later on, he said God would restore the years that those have taken. Well, that's just the way the church was destroyed back there, so it came back in a gradual fashion. Martin Luther was followed by various others namely John Calvin, Lee Fox, and various others in their day, and until about the middle of the nineteenth century (that would be in the 1850s), some of the nominal churches began to see holiness in the Bible. When they saw it, they began to preach holiness and they were called the Holiness Church. Among them, just to name a few, were the Mennonites, the Carmelites, the Brethren of the Pilgrim Holiness, the Free Methodist, and many others and they preached holiness. There is no such thing as holiness without the Holy Ghost but thank God they saw and set their standards from what they saw in the Bible, and from their own conscience.

When it came to the subject of dress, they set their standards from the Victorian age back in the last half of the nineteenth century. The women's skirts had to sweep the

---

[8] See Steinmetz's (2001) work on Reformers in the Wings.

floor and their sleeves had a band around their wrist and a ruffle below that. Women were even required at a time, when they were doing their washing using the old tub and washboard method, to wear long sleeves. Why? They were in their own house behind closed doors, but who knows? A salesman might knock at the door and you might forget to pull your sleeves down and open the door and he sees your forearms (that's how strict they were). The V-necks of today also wouldn't get by. Even some of them (do you remember this?) wore collars that stood up, and stays, that held those collars on the neck until sometimes they looked like their head was stretched. That was the way people dressed back then and those were the standards they set.

It was among those who embraced holiness that God began to pour out the Holy Ghost; well at first it was just a little sprinkle. You know sometimes rain will come and it doesn't start out as heavy rain at first, just a little drizzle, maybe it'll sprinkle a little but, kind of ease up a little here, and little there, and gradually it'll become steady and before you know it you have a full-fledged cloudburst. It's the way the outpouring of the Holy Ghost was. The Early Rain began back in Jesus's day. In the 1890s, few people received the baptism of the Holy Ghost in England, Holland, Germany, and Denmark. We have no record of anyone having received the Holy Ghost in the United States before the turn of the century. An experience that happened to a man in Topeka, Kansas would change this.

There was a man named Charles Parham, a white man, who had a school in Topeka. He bought a building called "Stone's Folly." Stone was a millionaire who started to build himself a great castle but his money ran out and he never got it finished, that's why it's called his folly. Parham was able to acquire the building and set up a seminary. In December of 1900, Parham had to take a trip. It was at this time they began to see the baptism of the Holy Ghost with the evidence of speaking in tongues in the Bible. None of his students had the Holy Ghost so as Parham got ready for his trip he assigned his class some homework. They were to study the baptism of the Holy Ghost with evidence of speaking in tongues. When he returned from his journey it was the last day of December in 1900 and he asked his class, "what have you found out?" They said, "we have found, according to the scriptures, that every time an individual was filled with the Holy Ghost, they spoke in other languages as the Spirit gave utterance." He said, "that's what I was convinced of and what I was hoping you would find out." So, they had their service that night and at the close of the service, they began to tarry for the baptism of the Holy Ghost. Sometime past midnight it began to sprinkle and many of the class members were filled with the Holy Ghost; however, strangely enough, Parham himself was not filled with the Holy Ghost until a few months later. After that, the Holy Ghost began to fall (the rain began to come down), and Parham began to go through the State of Kansas preaching the baptism of the Holy Ghost. Now understand this, Parham and his students still believed in the Trinitarian Doctrine set forth by the Catholics as they had no light of anything other than they had the baptism of the Holy Ghost. It spread through the State of Kansas, it kind of leap-frogged over the State of Oklahoma (might have been a little sprinkle there; nothing to amount to anything), down into the State of Texas, and there in Texas was a "colored" man by the name of William J. Seymour who had previously had an accident and lost an eye. A one-eyed man, who it was said was so unkempt, never had a suit pressed, mostly didn't even have his shirts ironed, but was a humble man. God filled Seymour with the Holy Ghost, called him to the ministry and he began to preach, and he had great success.

A woman in Los Angeles heard of William Seymour and his great success in the ministry but didn't know that he had the Holy Ghost. So, she sent for him to come to Los Angeles for him to hold a revival. It's been reported that Seymour went to Los Angeles sometime between the late winter of 1905 and early spring of 1906. When he arrived in Los Angeles the woman found out that he had the baptism of the Holy Ghost so, she put a padlock on her door and would not let Seymour in. There he was in a strange town without a penny in his pocket and he didn't know which way to go or turn. William Seymour prayed and as he was walking down the street, a white man met him, spoke with him, and said, "you come to my home on Bonnie Brae Street and I will give you a bed to sleep. It's important to make note of the race of these characters due to the era of events. The U.S. was racially divided during that period. Further, the man said to Seymour, "you will eat at my table and you can hold your services in my living room." The man never sought out compensation for his kindness towards Seymour, and that's just how God works. Well, he began to hold services in that living room and so many people began to come in and get filled with the Holy Ghost until it wasn't long before you couldn't even get in that house because it was too full.

Eventually, Seymour began to look around for a place and he found an abandoned Methodist church that more recently had been used as a livery stable where they kept horses. They went in, cleaned it up and started having service there and that's what is known today as the Azusa Street Mission. I have known many who were saved in that mission that year. I have preached to many of them, and I have had some of them (two of them at least) hold meetings for me in Kalamazoo in my church some years ago. So, I can go back there (not firsthand anyway) because I was not born until the early 1900s. But I knew those who were there and were saved in that meeting. I had personal contact with them, and

45

I have personally gleaned some historical knowledge from them.

God began to pour out the Holy Ghost in that place and they soon outgrew it and they had to get a larger place. It started a revival that continued through the city of Los Angeles for three years in which 10,000 or more people were filled with the Holy Ghost. Big churchmen (this was buzzed about abroad like it was on the Day of Pentecost) from all over the United States converged in Los Angeles to hear and to see this great thing. Most of them went back home and saying "it's of the devil" and spoke against it. A few of them believed and accepted it but generally, they rejected it, and from that time on they began to fight the baptism of the Holy Ghost and continued to do so until a few years ago when God showed them by pouring out the Holy Ghost right in their churches and universities. It is estimated that there are over 200,000 Catholics filled with the Holy Ghost in this country today. There have been more than 1,100 people filled with the Holy Ghost University of Notre Dame in South Bend, Indiana. So the church world had to realize that this is of God, after all, that's why you're not getting persecuted nowadays. They stopped fighting us, but at any rate here we have them now and they're all together, just one body, one people – black, white, red, brown, yellow--all the five colors of the human family. Male and female, young and old, educated and ignorant, rich and poor; all of them just one body in Christ and for a period of time it continued like that.

~7~

PART I: HISTORY

HISTORY OF THE P.A.W.

The Pentecostal Assemblies of the World was founded during the Azusa Street Mission in the year 1906 in Los Angeles, California. They had their first business meeting in 1907 which coincidentally was the year I was born. Unfortunately, accurate records and meeting minutes were not kept as we do today. There are only a few records of minutes between 1907 and 1919, but detailed records and minutes are available from 1919 until today. From 1906 to 1913, there was just one organization and the members were all one body, and that organization was called Pentecostal Assemblies of the World; however, the organization was not officially incorporated during that time.

In 1913, members of the organization were Pentecostal in experience but still believed in the Doctrine of the Trinity. Eventually, the members began to see the wonders of the Godhead in Jesus Christ and, consequently, baptism in the name of Jesus Christ for the remission of sins (Acts 2:4) caused great conflict in the infancy stage of the organization. Some members accepted baptism in Jesus as part of the plan of salvation, whereas others denounced the idea. Scripture says, *If we walk in the light as he is in the light, we have fellowship one with another, and the blood of Jesus Christ his Son cleanses us from all sin* (1 John 1:7). What makes it a fellowship? While some were in the light, others were not. We need to be walking in the light as Christ is in the light. Meaning, the light that He is in today, not the light that He was in 1906, in 1940, or the light that He shed on our pathway in 1970 but the light that He embodies today. If we walk in the light we will have fellowship with each other. I want you to know the church has been growing in knowledge from that day until now.

In 1913, the emphasis of baptism in the name of Jesus Christ infiltrated this Trinitarian organization but many of the members rejected it causing a great conflict. Hence, the first organizational split transpired in 1914. Those who refused to walk in the light that was shed on their pathway resigned from the Pentecostal Assemblies of the World (P.A.W.) and founded Trinitarian churches. Who were these groups? The African American members founded Church of God in Christ and the Caucasian members established Assemblies of God. The divisions have continued until the late 1970s. Many other organizations were erected from these ongoing divisions of which I would not name at this time. Members of these organizations received the baptism of the Holy Ghost, but they denounced baptism in the name of Jesus. The trend that caused the division continued until 1979. As the division continued, the splits have merged, and merges have split until there are over 130 Pentecostal organizations in the world today as of 1990. Clearly, every Pentecostal organization is able to trace its origin one way or another back to the Pentecostal Assemblies of the World.

When one talks about the parent-body, the P.A.W.is the parent body organization and the rest of them are the children. However, the parent body should not brawl with the children. I am a father of twelve children, I raised my children, and they're all married and have their own homes and families. I'm not asking them to come back home but I want to keep the avenues of communication open so that my wife and I can visit them and likewise, they can visit us at times. Who said because my children left home, they're no longer my children or they don't belong to my family anymore? Wouldn't that be foolish? But it's exactly what has transpired among the divided organizations. For years, Pentecostal organizations have separated, and the fragmented groups battled one another. Scripture says, *a house divided against itself cannot stand. Is Christ divided?* (Matthew 12:25; 1 Corinthians 1:13) It's time for us to leave fighting one another and recognize the universal body of Christ particularly among Pentecostal Apostolic.

The first organizational separation from the Pentecostal Assemblies of the World nearly destroyed it. In 1915, the Pentecostal Assemblies of the World was reorganized at a convention held in Indianapolis, Indiana in a church pastored by the late Bishop Garfield Thomas Haywood. Originally, the P.A.W. headquarter was located in Portland, Oregon, but the organization was not incorporated. In 1919, the late Bishop Robert Clarence Lawson left the Pentecostal Assemblies of the World mainly on two doctrinal issues. The first issue stemmed from the subject, marriage and divorce, and the second issue involved the existence of female preachers. He did not endorse the idea of women preachers. He did not believe if you were divorced and remarried before you were saved that you could be the recipient of salvation without leaving that current spouse and returning to the former spouse. On these two doctrinal points, he left the P.A.W.to establish the Church of Our Lord Jesus Christ Refuge Temple. Later, Bishop Lawson's new-found organization experienced disunion by one of his followers and the Bibleway Worldwide was birthed under the leadership of the late Bishop Smallwood Williams. Various other splits from Church of Our Lord Jesus Christ Refuge Temple were formed. These organizational disunions initiated the trend of divisions. The intent of this writing is not to cover all the organizational separations from the P.A.W. but to name a few of the major ones.

While it's notable that Bishop Lawson disassociated from the P.A.W. in 1919, it should be noted that something else happened that year as well; the Pentecostal Assemblies of the World headquarter was moved to Indianapolis, Indiana.

Ask ye of the Lord rain in the time of the latter rain; so the Lord shall make bright clouds, and give them showers of rain, to every one grass in the field. For the idols have spoken vanity, and the diviners have seen a lie, and have told false dreams; they comfort in vain: therefore they went their way as a flock, they were troubled, because there was no shepherd (Zechariah 10).

Notice the first word of the second sentence: "For" – gives the reason for the first sentence. And the reason ends up in the last clause, *because there was no shepherd.* When Jesus ministered in the flesh, He had compassion upon the people because they were as *sheep without a shepherd.* (Matthew 9:36). Why Jesus spoke with a sense of disappointment for the condition of His people? According to Jewish history, it is estimated that there were just over one thousand synagogues in Palestine in the days of Jesus and each synagogue had 24 officers or teachers. Knowing there were at least 24,000 teachers in Israel but there was no one qualified as a shepherd. Hence, the disappointment for the people who were badly in need of shepherd or a guide.[9]

It was necessary that the Latter Rain should fall because idol teachers and preachers have spoken falsely, diviners have seen a lie, and the prophets have misled the people of God. They comforted in vain; there just wasn't any ability to comfort. I think you may remember in the Books of Leviticus and Jeremiah, they had no comforter. This was the situation that existed; there was no comforter; and so, they went their way as a flock and no satisfaction? Why? Because there was no shepherd. Simply that God had no ministers on the scene. No one could bring people the truth. So, the Lord's admonishment is, *Ask ye of the Lord rain in the time of the latter rain* (Zechariah 10:1).

---

[9] See Tyson's The Early Pentecostal Revival.

When we talk about *Apostolic Roots*, the movement began with the apostles on the day of Pentecost (Book of Acts, 2). When did the Pentecostal roots begin during the latter rain? The latter rain represents the current church age and it began approximately in the turn of the century in 1906 during the Azusa Street Mission in Los Angeles, California. , the rain began to sprinkle sporadically in various countries for 10 to 15 years before. But, the P.A.W. based its inception from the time that the sprinkle was over and the rain began to fall in 1906. Scripture says, *so the Lord shall make bright clouds, and give them showers of rain, to every one grass in the field (Zechariah 10:1)*.

The original building of the Azuza Street Mission is no longer around, but just a little winding street in old Los Angeles. But in this crusade God began to pour out the Holy Ghost in such abundance that it wasn't too long after the service attendees outgrew the building capacity and had to find other places of worship.

The P.A.W. was birthed and the first business meeting was conducted in 1907. Business meeting were conducted from 1907 to 1919; however, meeting minutes were not appropriately kept. There were only have a brief record of minutes on file and one of the individuals with such information was the late General Secretary of the organization, Elder Robert F. Tobin. I wrote a letter to Elder Tobin and asked for the information because World War II was on the horizon and realized that some members of the P.A.W. would be going into the army. The document and the organizational record were important in seeking conscientious objections from participation in the war. It was Elder Tobin who passed it on to me around the year 1940. And for many years, it appeared I was the only guardian of the information when Elder Tobin had passed on. Since that period, the P.A.W. has kept its minute books up to date.

Saint Luke was a Gentile Christian under the pastoral leadership of Apostle Paul. He provided an account of the history of the New Testament church as outlined in the Book of Acts years after these events took place. He said, *those things which I most surely believed among us as they that were eye witnesses delivered to him (Luke 1:1-2).* The initial business meetings of the Pentecostal Assemblies of the World were held in the year of 1907 and that happened to be the year I was born. Hence, it's evident I was not on hand during those business meetings, but I collected the information from those who were at the meetings and I had personal contact with those who were part of the Azusa Street Mission. I have preached to a number of them who came to the Azusa Street Mission, and I have hosted ministers who were originally part of the Azusa Street Mission at my local church in Kalamazoo, Michigan. So, you may consider the information in this book to be quite authentic.

When the P.A.W. was founded there was one doctrine throughout the entire association, the doctrine of Trinity. The concept of Trinity or God in three persons (Father, Son, and Holy Ghost) has become an embedded tradition in nearly every Christian doctrine. Its inception dates back around the third century after the day of Pentecost. History informs us the Council of Nicaea essentially introduced the Nicene Creed in 325 A.D[10]. As Christians embraced the doctrine of Trinity then the doctrine of Oneness slowly became overshadowed and ultimately, the New Testament church entirely went into complete darkness over a period of hundreds of years. So, the sole light God left behind was just one organization on the face of the earth called Pentecostal Assemblies of the World.

---

[10] See Herman (2017). Fundamentals of Pentecostal Oneness.

Perhaps one of the most important planks in the Pente-costal Apostolic belief is the teaching of the oneness of God also known as the "Jesus only" message. The doctrine identi-fies those that believe this message as Apostolic. The strict and absolute unity of God is the first principle of the Bible. The entire scope and spirit of both the Old and New Testa-ments are distinctly on the side of the uni-personality of God. The Jews who made Monotheism their boast and glory never charged Christ or the first teachers of Christianity with originating any new theory of the God head. Christ and the apostles spoke of the Father as the only true God. It is re-peatedly admitted by Trinitarians that the word "Trinity" is not in the Bible; and that in the earliest records of Christian writings, not only is the word Trinity not found, but no equivalent of the word nor any proposition that characterizes God as three persons.

The Pentecostal Assemblies of the World was not incor-porated until 1919, but the association functioned with very little because of the unity among the members. There were problems, of course, but nothing that had anything to do with racial, national origins, or ethnic groups. In 1913, God began to reveal himself in parts and, ultimately, He revealed the oneness of the Godhead in Christ. Consequently, baptism in the name of Jesus for the remissions of sins led to a great conflict among members of the association. Many of them said it was a doctrine of devils. For instance, there was a case in Kalamazoo, Michigan where one of our members went to an Assemblies of God church service one evening and during the testimonial service, he shared that Jesus was God. Further, he informed the congregation that he was bap-tized in the name of Jesus Christ for the remission of sins. They called him down to the pulpit. He was under the im-pression he was summoned to address the congregation about his new experience but surprisingly once he was up-front, they put him down on his knees and prayed to cast that

"Jesus only" doctrine out of him. This was the attitude that many had, that this doctrine must be of the devil.

The late Bishop Garfield Thomas Haywood was a pioneer during the development of the P.A.W. history. When he first heard of the "Jesus only" message he likewise believed it was of the devil and denounced it. The story goes, Bishop Haywood came across a particular scripture, Jesus spoke then He went and hid himself (John 8:57-59). Bishop Haywood said, "Lord you will never hide yourself from me." After the revelation, he was baptized in the name of Jesus. Bishop Haywood had one of the largest churches (Christ Temple Church) in the City of Indianapolis, Indiana and after his conversion he immediately re-baptized all of his current congregates in the name of Jesus Christ.

One of the brethren from Arkansas attempted to forewarn Bishop Haywood about the new heresy-baptism in the name of Jesus Christ through a written letter. It stated, "I have learned that they of this new issue were coming your way and we wanted to warn you against them." Bishop Haywood responded to the letter with his own note, "you are too late. I have already accepted the doctrine and have been baptized in Jesus's name for the remission of my sins, and have baptized my people over again in the name of Jesus Christ." Incidentally, my current pastor in Kalamazoo, Michigan, Bishop Harry Herman's mother, one of the original members re-baptized by Bishop Haywood, received the Holy Ghost in 1913. Her name is Sister Harper Herman and she is the second oldest member of Christ Temple Church.

CHURCH OF GOD IN CHRIST

Charles H. Mason

The new doctrine of baptism caused a great division. And for approximately one year, the battle raged over the following question: "is there one God or are there three persons in the Godhead?" In 1914, those who had refused to walk in this new light had enough, so they left the P.A.W. fellowship. Following their separation; they had a convention and established Trinitarian organizations and churches. Among the former African-Americans members, the Church of God in Christ (COGIC) was formed and the former Caucasians members formed the Assemblies of God. Ultimately, each organization split until there exist a number of organizations, but all of these new organizations originated from the Pentecostal Assemblies of the World. Including, the Holy Spirit-filled Trinitarians churches and organizations. The only excerpt to this narrative, of all the churches that are in existence today that came from the Trinitarians, the Church of God in Christ is the only one that predated the Pentecostal Assemblies of the World as an organization before its Pentecostal experience. Otherwise, the founding members of the Church of God in Christ were associated with the PAW and shared the Holy Spirit experience with us from 1906 to 1914. So, when I say that every organization of Holy Ghost-filled people in the world today can connect their origins one way or another to the P.A.W. frankly, COGIC is the only association that may argue they predate the PAW. The organization pre-dated the PAW in name but in Pentecostal experience, they were with us for eight years before they withdrew and reestablished the Church of God in Christ.

Jesus prayed that they all may be one and look at what we've done (John 17:11). We have done everything else except what we should have done, so now we are attempting to reunite but we will speak more about this later in the book. The COGIC separation was the first and major split from the PAW as a Trinitarian organization. Afterward, the Pentecostal Assemblies of the World was then organized in Indianapolis, Indiana at Bishop Garfield Thomas Haywood's church in the year of 1915 with its headquarter established in Portland, Oregon. The P.A.W. reorganized as a "Jesus only oneness group."

CHURCH OF OUR LORD JESUS CHRIST

In 1919, the P.A.W. realized it's second major rift as an organization but its first as an oneness organization by the late Bishop Robert Clarence Lawson. He simply was unable to get along with Bishop G.T. Haywood. He contended against Bishop Haywood and he split from the P.A.W. on two points of doctrine. The first issue stemmed from the subject, marriage and divorce and the second issue involved the existence of female preachers. There was a time when Bishop Haywood did not believe you could be saved unless you dissolved that second marriage. One of Bishop Haywood's relatives, I believe it was his nephew, came into

57

Bishop Haywood's service and stood up one night to be baptized. But he had been divorced, and was remarried and Bishop Haywood refused to baptize him because he said he was living in adultery, and he could not be baptized unless he severed that marriage. The young man did not dissolve the current marriage and he continued to come to church, and on a Sunday night as he was sitting in the service while Bishop Haywood was preaching the Lord poured out the Holy Ghost on his nephew, and right in the middle of the service he began to speak in other tongues as the Spirit of God gave him utterance. And Bishop Haywood, like Peter, said "who am I that I could resist God" and finally baptized him in Jesus's name. Hence, from that moment the congregation realized that the marriage was not a prerequisite for salvation. When one comes into the house of God, the person comes under God's law and no prior experience can interfere with God's plan to fill one with the Holy Spirit and for the person to be baptized. When one arrives in the church he or she is accepted as he or she comes. But Bishop Lawson (he was not a bishop at that time) did not agree with that school of thought and decided to disassociate himself from Bishop Haywood. Formerly from Columbus, Ohio, he separated and founded Refuge Church of Christ which later became the Church of Our Lord Jesus Christ (COOLJC) and set up his headquarters in New York City.

When Bishop Lawson separated from Bishop Haywood his organization set out to destroy the memory of Bishop Haywood. Consequently, there were several churches in the Pentecostal Assemblies of the World, primarily those from eastern United States, set out to destroy the memory of Bishop Haywood. In fact, there are Pentecostal Assemblies of the World churches that have not heard of Bishop Haywood. Later, Church of Our Lord Jesus Christ experienced a division because Bishop Lawson refused to elevate other church leaders as bishops. He was the head and called himself an apostle. Biblically, it's error to assume the title "apostle" because there are no such positions in the current dispensation of the church. The office of apostleship ended with the death of the apostles, so the highest office in the church today is bishop. He assumed the title apostle—not only that, he was referred to as the chief apostle. The only chief apostle I am aware of has a different name, and his name is Jesus Christ. For He is the apostle of our profession, he is the Chief Apostle (Hebrews 3:1).

BIBLEWAY CHURCH WORLDWIDE

Bishop Smallwood E. Williams

There was a split in Bishop Lawson's organization that arose many years ago, headed by the general secretary of that organization, Bishop Smallwood Williams. He served as the general secretary under Bishop Lawson and led a division among COOLJC members to form another organization under the banner, the Bibleway Church Worldwide. Currently, Bishop Williams' organization is still in existence but the organization lost many churches to the Apostolic World Christian Fellowship. Bishop Williams made a number of bishops and this satisfied those who were clamoring for the office of bishop under Bishop Robert C. Lawson. So, through Bishop Lawson's sorrow, he lost a good share of his organization by trying to enforce the one-man rule.

The Lord never endorsed a one-man church, or an organization built around the personality of one man at any time.

Because when that man is gone it's going to dishevel the organization. This leads me to Bishop Samuel N. Hancock of Bethlehem Temple in Detroit, Michigan. Bishop Hancock was like a father to me, and I loved him more than my own father. You may not be able to understand that but it's literally true. Bishop Hancock was responsible for rending a number of members from the P.A.W. as well. He, along with others, established the Pentecostal Churches of the Apostolic Faith.

FIRST P.A.W. OFFICERS

The first top officials of the Pentecostal Assemblies of the World were elected in 1912. The PAW was a fragmented association until that time. The top official was recognized as the general superintendent during the infancy stage of the organization. The term bishop was not introduced to the organization at this point. J. J. Frazee served as the first general superintendent and he was a white man. It's important to note his race during this period because it was not acceptable, according to social orders for Caucasians and African Americans to fellowship. From its beginning, the P.A.W. was a racially diverse faith-based organization. This is notable because at that time colored folks and Caucasians did not fellowship in the church, as a rule. Elder Frazee, the first general superintendent, served until he left the organization in 1918. We do not know what happened to him but we believe that he died in the influenza epidemic of that time. Consequently, there were two conventions held in 1918. During the first convention, general superintendent J.J. Frazee presided over the meetings. The second one that was held in October of that year had a different presiding general superintendent. It was E.W. Doak and he was also a white man. Ultimately, the leadership of the Pentecostal Assemblies of the World consisted of the following racially diverse leaders: the first two leaders were white; the next two were black; the next one was white, then the next one was black, and so on. The Pentecostal Assemblies of the World has been one of the most racially integrated Christian organizations from its inception; however, over the years and through the splits, the Caucasians representation has dwindled.

In 1918, Elder E.W. Doak succeeded J.J. Frazee and he continued in that role until the year 1925. Note, each of the elected officials served for approximately seven years. Finally, the Pentecostal Assemblies of the World was incorporated in 1919 under the laws of the State of Indiana for the maximum term of 50 years. The incorporators were Elder E.W. Doak as the general superintendent, Elder Garfield Thomas Haywood, and Elder Daniel Charles Owen Opperman. G T. Haywood was an African-American, E. W. Doak was a Jewish brother, and D.C. Opperman was Caucasian. They were the three incorporators of the Pentecostal Assemblies of the World.

The organization continued until the year 1967 when the 50 years were about to expire. At that time, we were authorized to reincorporate under the new law of the State of Indiana that allowed the corporation to become perpetual. In the lifetime of Bishop Samuel Grimes, the law was passed that it should be done the following year, but during that next year Bishop Grimes expired and I became the presiding bishop of the P.A.W. So, it became one of my first official duties, along with my general secretary, Bishop James A. Johnson of St. Louis to complete the incorporation of the Pentecostal Assemblies of the World, Inc. When you read the P.A.W. minute Book of the incorporators, you will find both our names, and those names will be there as long as the Pentecostal Assemblies of the World, Inc. exists.

The title of bishop was first assumed by the Pentecostal Assemblies of the World in 1915 and there was a bishop board of five members. These five members consisted of the original bishop board and Brother Garfield Thomas Haywood was elected as the first Presiding Bishop of the Pentecostal Assemblies of the World. I admit that Bishop Haywood was the man who inspired my ministry. I got my start in my ministry both preaching and teaching under his tutelage and it is of my opinion that he was the man who received more revelation of God in those days than any other man. Bishop Haywood was the pioneer of the oneness message. The revelations he shared created the knowledge of separation between the Trinitarian message and the oneness of the Godhead message. There were other Pentecostal oneness preachers and teachers in those days but Bishop Haywood was the man that Trinitarians recognized as the pioneer. Saint Paul said,

> *According to the grace of God which is given unto me, as a wise master-builder, I have laid the foundation, and another buildeth there on. But let every man take heed how he buildeth there on. Now if any man building upon this foundation, of gold, silver, precious stones, wood, hay and stubble; every man's work shall be made manifest: for the day shall declare it, because it shall be revealed by fire* (1 Corinthians 3:10-13).

The writer is using a parable about the construction of a building to explain a biblical concept. You may think then of the gold, silver, precious stones, wood, hay, and stubble as the types of material that the builder would use. But this is the wrong conclusion. Paul's metaphor is referring to the soul of men. The building project is not about the usage of materials for a new building. The parable is referring to the quality of the workmanship of the builder rather than his materials. The Trinitarians had a saying associated with the previous verse: "we are building with gold, and silver and precious stones but they say they (referring to the oneness) are building on Hay-wood and stubble." Note, the play on words by the Trinitarians, "wood, hay, and stubble"; they reversed the first two words to get the name Haywood. So, I just want you to realize that those who hold to the Trinitarian persuasion recognized the fact that Bishop Haywood was practically the pioneer of the oneness movement.

Bishop Haywood was a preacher of par excellence. God gave him more revelation than any other man. He served as presider of the Pentecostal Assemblies of the World for seven years until his demise.

PENTECOSTAL MINISTERIAL ALLIANCE

The year 1924 was a turbulent period for the P.A.W. The organization was faced with its first major racial divide. I assume that the African-American brethren were not the cause of the racial rift but the white brethren of the organization. The Caucasian members of the organization felt that their social status was at risk of being rubbished for having the names of African-American men on their ecclesiastical credentials. Many of the whites that were in contention with the black brethren were primarily brethren from the southern region of the United States. Obviously during this period there existed a tension between blacks and whites in the South. Ultimately, the majority of the white brethren seceded from the P.A.W. and formed another organization. They formed an organization called the Pentecostal Ministerial Alliance, and then later reincorporated under a new name, Pentecostal Church Incorporated. They called themselves a "lily white" organization, and no African-American was permitted to be in that organization.

I'm not blaming my white brethren but I put the blame where it belongs--to the devil. It's important to remember that the devil is our adversary and I am not ignoring of his devices. The only blames I could put on the white brethren was that they were intoxicated away by this persuasion. They were weak when they should have been strong, and it caused this separation.

When Bishop Haywood died in 1931 it was a devastating blow to the PAW. It is believed that the ill will from the brethren on the East Coast of the United States caused Bishop Haywood to die from a broken heart. He died because he did not want to live. When he was ill, he refused to rest due to his arduous ecclesiastical work and his ministerial commitment to the island of Jamaica. When he returned from Jamaica his illness exacerbated and he never recovered. When he returned from Jamaica he took to his bed and he stayed there, but he could not die. Finally, he said to Bishop Hancock, "Brother Sam, tell the brethren to stop praying for me, let me go." We stopped praying and God took him home. The cruelty and the ungodliness of people in the P.A.W. caused him to depart this life sooner than his time. My tears get very close to the surface every time I think or speak of it.

When the convention met the year of Bishop Haywood's death, the East Coast (United States) delegates were afraid that Bishop Hancock would succeed Bishop Haywood and they would have a second Haywood. So, under the guise of honoring Bishop Haywood, which they didn't intend to do at all, the coalition from the eastern region of the U.S. made a resolution that passed on the floor, saying in honor of Bishop Haywood, the office of presiding bishop should be open for one year. This meant that for one year they would rotate the gavel among the bishops.

PART I: HISTORY

PENTECOSTAL ASSEMBLIES OF JESUS CHRIST

After the death of Bishop Haywood in 1931, there was an organization called the Apostolic Churches of Jesus Christ (ACJC). The group and the Pentecostal Assemblies of the World attempted a merger that year. Both organizations proposed conditions under which they would accept a merge. During both organizations' respective conventions, the merger was rejected because neither one was willing to make a concession on their terms. Naturally, it was assumed the merger proposal was defeated. On the contrary, in September 1931, many of the leaders of both organizations met in St. Louis, Missouri to conclude the merger. After the merger was official, the Pentecostal Assemblies of Jesus Christ was founded. Bishop Samuel N. Hancock, Bishop John Silas Holly, Bishop Karl Smith, and many other of the brethren of the Pentecostal Assemblies of the World went with the Pentecostal Assemblies of Jesus Christ.

This is when I came into the picture. I had been in the ministry for a couple of years at that time, but I had no credentials with any organization. My pastor went into Pentecostal Assemblies of Jesus Christ (PAJC). Bishop Hancock was my mentor, a man dearer to me than my father. He was my pastor and the title bishop was not in use during that period. I came into the Pentecostal Assemblies of Jesus Christ and was ordained in that organization in the year 1936 in Bishop Karl Smith's church in Columbus, Ohio. The same year I learned about the position of the Pentecostal Assemblies of Jesus Christ on racial issues. The majority of the members of the organization believed in segregation. Hence, they came up with the proposition that the African-American brethren would have their convention meanwhile the white brethren would have their elsewhere. However, possibly once in seven years, both racial groups would come together in a joint convention somewhere in the northern part of the

U.S. where the organization will not face tensions. As a young pastor, I said to myself *"that can't be God"* then I walked away from the PAJC. For the following two years I was independent, not because I believed in being independent but I wanted to know that when I made my next move, it would be my last. So, I used the time to explore and studied t various oneness organizations. Ultimately, I found the Pentecostal Assemblies of the World to be the original organization, the parent body--the father of all the children. Further, it was the one organization that held more closely to the apostolic doctrines though, it was imperfect. I learned it was still an interracial organization. In 1938, I joined the Pentecostal Assemblies of the World and I expect to stay until I die or until the Lord calls us all home.

The Pentecostal Assemblies of Jesus Christ was formed, but it was an unlawful merger because both organizations had voted against it. The intent of the merger was to disband the Apostolic Churches of Jesus Christ and the Pentecostal Assemblies of the World, and have one organization–the Pentecostal Assemblies of Jesus Christ. The merger was unsuccessful because both the Apostolic Churches of Jesus Christ and the Pentecostal Assemblies of the World retained their independent status but the attempt almost destroyed the membership of the Pentecostal Assemblies of the World.

When Bishop Lewis came on the scene there were only two of the original bishops left on the P.A.W. leadership. These were Bishop Floyd. I. Douglas and Bishop Arthur William Lewis. These two men began a campaign to reunite the brethren that left the P.A.W. as a result of the merger. Bishop Douglas partially traveled because of his health problems. He had asthma so he did not travel as much as Bishop Lewis and the others. Bishop Lewis traveled with a few of the brethren who remained with the Pentecostal Assemblies of the World. The small group of P.A.W. leaders met and authorized Bishop Lewis to select an elder to assist him. He selected a man by the name of Samuel K. Grimes and they traveled together throughout the year. They recovered a number of those who were formerly in the Pentecostal Assemblies of the World.

During the 1932 convention, the Pentecostal Assemblies of the World was reorganized-not reincorporated. Also during the same convention, a new president bishop was to be named and Elder Grimes was chosen. It's important to note, the new presiding bishop would have been Bishop Arthur William Lewis, but due to health challenges, he endured for a 10-year period. He was unable to preach a sermon and ultimately remained out of sight. I visited him on various occasions in his very serious illness. It was his good friend Elder A. C. Baker of Portland, Oregon, who rescued him and put him on a special diet that brought him out of his illness. Again, because of his illness he was out of the picture and Elder Samuel Grimes, who was the disciple of Bishop Lewis so, naturally, he was elevated to the office of president bishop was the next leader. Bishop Grimes was elected to a four-year term but he served as Presiding Bishop for 15 years (1932 to 1947). There was never a re-election process so he just continued as presiding bishop unlawfully.

In 1947, Elder J. E. Collins of Texas filed a suit of dissolution against the Pentecostal Assemblies of the World, because he had learned they were not operating according to their by-laws. He brought it to the attention of some of the leaders and they just laughed at him, saying it didn't mean a thing. So, the only way he knew how to get our attention was to file a suit of dissolution and that would have happened in 1947. The Pentecostal Assemblies of the World would have been lost with all of the assets being claimed by the State of Indiana. According to the law, the charter required an election of the Board of Directors annually and there had not been an election for 21 years. Frankly, the organization was operating contrary to its charter and it would have been dissolved if the action had not been corrected. . The Board of Directors was elected, and it was agreed in advance that the member receiving majority votes would assume the presiding bishop position.

The nominees for the office of Presiding Bishop were as follow: Bishop Grimes and Bishop Hancock, and Bishop Grimes won by a landslide. There were two nominees for assistant presiding bishop office: Bishop David Schultz and Bishop Paddock. I won by a larger majority. So, for 14 years I served under Bishop Grimes and we worked together as father and son until his death. It was in that election that I was elected to the Board and I have been a member of the Board since that time. I served as the vice-chairman for 14 years, and chairman of the Board of Directors for seven years. I was not only a director but I was in the top offices for 21 years.

The results of the election during that period were as follows Bishop Grimes received 208 votes; the second closest was Bishop Karl Smith with 204 votes. Bishop Grimes was elected in 1932 for a four-year term but he served until 1953. We have since amended our bylaws to a three-year term. In 1953, we had an election and we've had a regular election ever since. Also in that year, a new office was created. This was the office of the assistant presiding bishop.

UNITED PENTECOSTAL CHURCH

In the year of 1945, the Pentecostal Assemblies of Jesus Christ and the Pentecostal Churches, Inc. merged to form the United Pentecostal Church (UPC). The United Pentecostal Church is the largest Apostolic or Oneness Pentecostal organization in the world. It is much larger in members than the Pentecostal Assemblies of the World and it's predominantly a racially white organization. I have their original Minute Book and there is a section in the back of the book called a *colored branch* where the African-American ministers and their organizations are separately listed as the colored ministers. Now, as a white minister, I couldn't quite understand why my African-American brethren would accept a situation like that. After reviewing the names listed in the said section, and I discovered that most of them had been former worshippers with the Pentecostal Assemblies of the World or some other organization and were just looking for a place to rest. I tell you this; to this day the United Pentecostal Church is not an integrated organization. What I'm telling you is that they have many good men, but overall as an organization they are rotten to the core. They don't like me because of my stance on bigotry but I have to say it. I did not completely stop fellowshipping with the United Pentecostal Church brethren, but I do not fellowship with the United Pentecostal Church organization. I've been to their organization and they've come to ours. When they would attend our functions, we would stop everything and acknowledge them, put badges on them, give them a chance to address the organization, whether it was a business or religious subject, and even had them preach at our conventions. For instance, Bishop Lawrence Brisbin and I went to a UPC convention and they didn't recognize or acknowledge our presence. Now, I think you can understand why I left the Pentecostal Assemblies of Jesus Christ when I did. You see, I can only believe what the Bible teaches me. There's just one body, and we are to be together and love as brethren.

After the United Pentecostal Church was formed in 1945, most of the white brethren that were left in the Pentecostal Assemblies of the World were recruited and enticed.

They were enticed by being offered office positions whereas others were offered money to help them build churches. Now, this isn't fake news because I have firsthand experience. In the UPC 1949 convention, they appointed a special committee to attend the P.A.W. convention solely to recruit white ministers and I was one of their targets. The committee met with me in that convention and we talked for about four hours and when the private meeting was adjourned my name became trash to them and it still is to this day. I asked, "why is it that we should not worship together?" And they said, "well, now if we're together it's only a matter of time until there will be intermarriages." Well, I don't deny that wouldn't happen but if you would like to know, I have quite an international family myself. As much as I know in my bloodline includes English, Irish, Welsh, Scotch, German, Dutch, Swiss, and French. Besides that, because of interracial marriages in my family, I have cousins almost everywhere in this country. The late Earl Fisher of Cleveland, Ohio, is my cousin. Evangelist Lorraine Willis of San Bernardino is my cousin as well. I have two nieces, both of them blondes who married African-American men and they have biracial children. This marriage tied Bishop Holly and me together because his nephew married my niece. Further, there is a family of eight children who call Elder Herman Patterson, Uncle Lou. It's the same family that calls me uncle because we are both uncles to that family. You see I can't say that there won't be any interracial marriage because that's none of my business. I chose the route I wanted and I expect every other man would do the same. If my wife should die and I should marry again I would make the choice then. Nobody would tell me who I could choose.

The committee disagreed with intermarriage and I said "give me a scripture against it," and they did. The Bible says, "doth not even nature itself teach you, that, it is a shame for a man to have long hair" (1 Corinthians 11). Well, they read the hair part of it and said nature itself teaches you some things saying "don't you know that animals don't mix?" and I replied, "maybe a dog and cat won't mix, but I know that you know, that some animals do. We get the tiger and the lions mix. Of course, there wouldn't be such a thing as a mule." There wasn't a word from them. But I continued, "maybe a dog and a cat don't mix, but I'll tell you what, if you put a black dog and a white dog, male and female, in the same yard, tell me what's going to happen. Or you take a black cat and white cats, male and female, put them in the same yard and tell me what's going to happen. Or you take a black rooster and a white hen, put them in the same yard and tell me what's going to happen". By the time we were done, I was a bad boy in their eyes. My name has been mud with the United Pentecostal Church since that time and frankly, I don't mind it the least. "If you suffer for righteousness sake, happy are ye" (1 Peter 3:14). They haven't made me suffer as that might be suffering to some because everybody likes to be respected and honored.

This is my honest account and experience with the UPC and I know because that committee was appointed at their convention to get me. If any of my readers are United Pentecostal Church members, I'm sorry because it's not my intention to harm but to shed light on wickedness. I will admit there are many good United Pentecostal Church brethren. Another experience, when the P.A.W. met in South Bend, Indiana, the United Pentecostal Church sent letters to all of their pastors around that neighborhood or that area, forbidding them to come to our convention. But many of them came anyway and when they came, we treated them just like we would anybody else. They are our brothers and sisters. If there's any breech in fellowship, it's because of sin. Now there's one thing noticeable that they've held onto in their doctrine over the years, and that is a minister may not have a television. There isn't anything in the Bible about a television. The closest thing you have in your Bible is this: *they that use this world is not abusing it* (1 Corinthians 7:13). So, the television is of the world, and if you use it, as long as you do not abuse the use of it there's nothing wrong. But the Bible does say, *to have respect of persons is to commit sin* (James 2:9). Prejudice for any reason, racial or otherwise, the Bible says is sin and the very foundation of that organization is built on sin.

PENTECOSTAL CHURCHES OF APOSTOLIC FAITH

Bishop Samuel N. Hancock
Founder

After some time, Bishop Samuel Hancock, along with many of the other black brethren, returned to the Pentecostal Assemblies of the World in the early part of 1938. After their return, among those who were restored to the office of bishop in the Pentecostal Assemblies of the World were Bishop Hancock, Bishop Karl Smith, and Bishop John S. Holly. In 1957, Bishop Samuel N. Hancock and Elder Willie Lee, the pastor of Christ Temple in Indianapolis, met and formed a new organization called the Pentecostal Churches of Apostolic Faith (PCAF). Subsequently, Bishop Hancock became the presiding bishop and Elder Lee was elevated to the office of bishop and became the assistant presiding bishop. This continued until the death of Bishop Hancock. After the death of Bishop Hancock, Bishop Lee attempted to assume the leadership role of the organization and he found that the majority of the members didn't want him, and this caused great conflict and some divisions took place in the PCAF. There isn't a year that goes by that there aren't more splits. I don't know how many groups have come out of that unfortunate situation. Many of them are in the Apostolic World Christian Fellowship. We hold nothing against them at all, we have good fellowship.

Willie Lee

APOSTOLIC WORLD CHRISTIAN FELLOWSHIP

W.G. Rowe

In May 1970, the Apostolic World Christian Fellowship (AWCF) was formed by Worthy G. Rowe. It is not another organization but in namesake, it's an association of Oneness Pentecostal organizations. Its principal purpose is to fulfill the prayer of Jesus in the 17th chapter of the Book of John, *that they all may be one* (John 17:21). According to the association bylaws, any organization desiring to affiliate with the Apostolic World Christian Fellowship is required to sign a letter of intent. When a major organization signs a letter of intent, all of its members can become affiliated and become a card-carrying member of the Apostolic World Christian Fellowship. Currently, I am affiliated with the organization as the vice chairman and I have served for three terms.

In 1969, the year before the incorporation to AWCF, the Pentecostal Assemblies of the World considered signing a letter of intent but due to the uncertainty of the potential impact on our organization, we decided to explore the matter before committing to the idea. So, the PAW appointed a committee to investigate and report at the next convention which was in 1970. In 1970, the Pentecostal Assemblies of the World signed that letter of intent and I was authorized at the time as the presiding bishop along with Elder Paul Bowers as the secretary of the Pentecostal Assemblies of the World to represent our organization in the Apostolic World Christian Fellowship initial meeting. It was my privilege to preach the opening message in the first convention. Strangely, a couple of months later, Bishop Smallwood Williams of Bible way Churches Worldwide forfeited his association and had his meeting in Bishop William L. Bonner's church in New York City, New York. Members of the P.A.W. were requested to have representation at the Bible way Churches Worldwide first convention and yours truly had the privilege of preaching the opening message as well.

There were 46 of the 130 Oneness Pentecostal organizations signed up as affiliates of the A.W.C.F. by 1980. When the Pentecostal Assemblies of the World convention is in session, we're there principally for business, but when the Apostolic World Christian Fellowship conference is in session we're there for fellowship, and you'll see the love of God on display in a manner that no other organization has thereof. We may or may not be conscious of the organization, but to the other brothers and sisters in this world, it makes a difference because we need to know each other.

During one occasion at the World Fellowship conference, I was seated at the head of the table and I noticed the next two chairs immediately to my right were vacant. Then, the next two adjacent to those chairs became occupied by two African-American brethren of other organizations. I thought the two chairs to my immediate right were reserved for somebody else. Eventually, I called a waitress and asked, "is there something wrong with these chairs that nobody's sitting in them?" Then before she can answer, the brethren in the next chair said to me, "oh! Bishop Paddock, we thought maybe some of your people would becoming so, we left those seats open for them". And I replied saying, "what are you talking about? These *are* my people." Soon after, they got up and moved toward me and sat down with us. This is the kind of fellowship that is encouraged within the Apostolic World Christian Fellowship. It shouldn't make any difference what organization a man belongs to, but the few requirements are that one is baptized in the name of Jesus Christ, have the baptism of the Holy Ghost with speaking in tongues, and believe in a holy lifestyle. We have at the time of this writing 46 different Apostolic organizations that have joined and we're working on the rest of them. I'm hopeful that we could get all the Apostolic organizations, although I doubt that we ever will. The order of these last days is not to split, divide, separate, or make new organizations*, but gather yourselves together. Yea, gather together saith the Lord* (Zephaniah 2:1). It's the message for the day that precedes the coming of the Lord and for His church, the body of Christ.

I have given you a brief history of the Pentecostal Assemblies of the World up to this time. I served as an assistant presiding bishop under Bishop Grimes for 14 years, and at the time of his passing, I was elevated to the office of presiding bishop, which left the office of assistant presiding bishop vacant. By the nomination and election, there were three who were nominated. By election, the late Bishop Frank

Bowden was elected to serve as my assistant, and for the seven years I served as presiding bishop while he served as assistant presiding bishop. When I ceased to be the presiding bishop, he was nominated again but he sent word to the convention that met in Denver that year that he would not be able to be there because of illness. Ultimately, he asked that we not consider him for office at the time. Bishop Francis L. Smith of Akron, Ohio was elected presiding bishop (1974-1980), Bishop Lawrence C. Brisbin of Grand Rapids, Michigan was elected as the assistant presiding bishop and at the time of this writing, a new election will take place and neither Bishop Smith or Bishop Brisbin can run for their respective offices but they can each run for the other office. For instance, Bishop Smith could choose to run for the office of assistant presiding bishop and Bishop Brisbin can choose to run for the office of the presiding bishop. At this point, I don't have any idea who will be our next presiding bishop, but one thing I do know: when we get to Miami, Florida (if we're still here) in 1980 there will be an election and God will speak. The Bible said *the lot is cast into the lap and the whole disposing thereof is of the Lord* (Proverbs 16:33). It's God that directs the minds of people to cast their vote in the manner that will get the man or woman he wants in office.

After the 1974 PAW election in Denver and the report of the votes was made, I called Bishop Francis Smith to stand beside me at the podium. I presented him with the gave land said to the congregation, "God has spoken and this is God's man, and he is the new presiding bishop because God has appointed him so." I also said, "it is my great privilege and pleasure to pass the gavel on to a man who is better than I."

I believe that because I believe in God's word. There was a time perhaps I would not have said that but the Lord has made me know it was not His will for me to continue. I didn't know why at that time and God does not always tell you why. Incidentally, my son, who was a very fine Christian member of the church in Kalamazoo, Michigan and his baby son were killed in a truck accident. When the news became public someone tried to comfort me and said, "we don't always know why God does what He does." I responded by saying, "we don't have to know why. That's God's business, not mine. He takes who He wishes. *The Lord gave, and the Lord hath taken away; blessed be the name of the Lord* (Job 1:21)[11]

---

[11] During the first printing of this Book, Lawrence C. Brisbin was elected presiding bishop with James A. Johnson as his assistant.

~ 8 ~

PART II: HISTORY

P.A.W. OFFICE OF BISHOPS

The year 1925 was a period when the Pentecostal Assemblies of the World begin the use of the title bishop. When it was used in the scripture, the title of bishop simply meant overseer. It is used in your Bible in two different manners: as overseer of a local church which would be the pastor, and as overseer of a district or diocese. The P.A.W. realized the problems that would be faced if the title bishop is used in any of these manners. Hence, the organization did not use the title of a bishop for a pastor. When you read 1 Timothy chapter 3, the author is addressing firstly, the role of a pastor and secondly, of a diocese. The Pentecostal Assemblies of the World only use the title of "Bishop" for a bishop of a district or diocese. In the New Testament, when you find the word bishop it is referred to as a pastor, so it would not be unlawful to use that title for a pastor, but as far as the P.A.W. is concerned it is not expedient, so we do not use it in that manner. I hope that will shed some light on the word bishop, so when I speak of a bishop you will not be thinking of a pastor but a bishop over a state or a region; a district or diocese.

During this writing, I was serving as the bishop of the Fifth Episcopal District of the Pentecostal Assemblies of the World, also known as the Northern District Council. The region or the district that I oversaw consists of the entire state of Michigan and a portion of Ontario, Canada. There are examples of other district councils that cover multiple state lines or regions such as the Midwestern District Council which covers part of the State of Illinois and the State of Missouri, whereas, other district councils such as the 6th Episcopal District of the Pentecostal Assemblies--the Illinois District Council--covers just part of the State of Illinois. A district council is also known as a diocese, and the spiritual leader or presiding officer of a diocese is known as a diocesan bishop. In some cases, the diocesan bishop is also the chairman of the district council as well. However, the diocesan and chairman role are two distinct responsibilities in a given district council. As long as I am Bishop of the Northern District Council, my vision will remain that the chairman of the council is responsible for the business operation of the council, while the bishop is responsible for the spiritual conduct of the council and all of its churches. I had the opportunity to teach a seminar in our council concerning the distinction between the two offices. Having the responsibility divided is much better than one person attempting to do it all alone. The best way to understand the separate functionality of diocesan bishop and chairman of the council is to compare the role of chairman of the board of a company and the role of president of the same company. The role of chairman of the board is typically separated from the role of president of the organization. The chairman of the board presides over the board's business but the president of the company serves as an ex-officio member of the board and presides over the daily operation of the company. However, there are organizations where the chairman of the board also serves as the president as well. I do not attempt to tell any other council how to conduct their business when I am invited to assist in other councils where the bishop of the diocese serves as both the diocesan and the chairman of the council.

At the beginning of assuming the title of bishop, the Pentecostal Assemblies of the World had laws that when a man was elevated or elected to the office of bishop he did not take office for one year. During that time he was under a character fitness investigation to see if he was qualified for the office. I felt that such law was a little strange because such due diligence should have been completed and the findings should have been made known before the person was elected. I never knew of an actual investigation being made other than that of the late

Bishop James Leo Sypes. In fact, I was holding a meeting for him during the period he was under investigation and I humorously told him I was there investigating him, which wasn't the case. It was customary to be elected then one had to wait a year before he could be seated, after which at that time or some future time be offered a diocese. In later years, that law was amended that the bishop could not be seated if there was no diocese available for him, and if none could be made then he couldn't be seated until he was given a diocese, so it could be two or three years after one was elected before he became seated as a bishop. Years later, we amended our laws so when one was elected as bishop, he was seated and given a diocese all at the same time frame. There is no longer a waiting period. Also, we have a law that after a bishop has successfully served for two years with no blemish on his record, he is then established as a bishop permanently, unless forfeited by misconduct the office is his for the rest of his life. If he should be overtaken in sin, then his bishopric would be taken from him.

There was an instance where we had to unfrock a bishop in Africa, not because he committed adultery, robbed a bank, or committed murder, but because his conduct was unbecoming of a clergyman in the Pentecostal Assemblies of the World. As overseer of a P.A.W. school, the said Bishop rejected the management decision of the Executive Board and, eventually, the court ceased the assets of the school. He took the P.A.W to court and the court decided in our favor. This was one example of various P.A.W. bishops that were disqualified. Later I will give you their names, when they were made bishop, how long they served, and what was the cause of the termination of their services.

THE FIRST BOARD OF BISHOPS

G.T. Haywood   G.B. Rowe   J.M. Turpin   A. F. Varnell   A.R. Schooler

In 1925, the Pentecostal Assemblies of the World assumed the title of a bishop for its superintendents and the board of Bishops was erected. The first board of bishops consisted of five men: Garfield Thomas Haywood, Glen Beecher Rowe, Joseph Marcel Turpin, Albert Franklin Varnell, and Alexander R. Schooler. This was the first and original Board of Bishops of the Pentecostal Assemblies of the World. It was at this time the top office was given the title of presiding Bishop and of these five men elected the first Presiding Bishop of the Pentecostal Assemblies of the World in the person of Bishop Garfield T. Haywood. Bishop Haywood served as presider until his demise in April 1931. G. B. Rowe and J.M. Turpin served in the office of bishops from 1925 and until 1931. Consequently, the Pentecostal Assemblies of Jesus Christ was founded illegally by drawing several members of the Pentecostal Assemblies of the World. In 1931, G.B. Rowe transitioned to the Pentecostal Assemblies of Jesus Christ and he never returned to the Pentecostal Assemblies of the World, whereas, J. M. Turpin was dismissed from his role as bishop. Shortly, he was reinstated not as a bishop but as a minister in the Pentecostal Assemblies of the World. His health declined rapidly within a short amount of time; weighing more than 300 pounds to under 100 pounds and soon thereafter he died.

Albert F. Varnell is the only one of the sixty-two bishops of the Pentecostal Assemblies of the World I personally did not know. I knew of him but not personally. The only thing I can tell you, he was a Caucasian fellow and he pastored a church somewhere in the central part of Illinois. In 1929, his service came to an end as a bishop in the Pentecostal Assemblies of the World, but I never knew the reason(s) why, perhaps he died during that time. Bishop Alexander R. Schooler's service ended in 1929 as well. Unfortunately, he was unfrocked. He was eventually restored to serve in ministry, but he never returned to the Pentecostal Assemblies of the World. He wrote some of songs that many of us have sung.

ELEVATION OF BISHOPS

In 1928, Bishop Arthur William Lewis was the first minister elevated to the office of bishop since the original five members of the Board of Bishops. Bishop Lewis served as a bishop of the organization until his passing in 1973. I had the privilege of preaching at his funeral. Arthur W. Lewis was made bishop and yet I preached far more years than he did and that sounds like a little difficult situation, doesn't it? Bishop Lewis had health challenges that prevented him from fully functioning in the ministry. There was a ten-year period where he was unable to preach due to health challenges. He still retained the title of bishop during that period but in an honorary capacity. After those ten years his health improved and he was restored as a full-fledged bishop of the Pentecostal Assemblies of the World and was offered the Pacific Northwest diocese.

He relocated to the region but neither he nor his wife could live in such a climate, so after a period of time it was asked of a young man by the name of Elder Benjamin (Benny) Moore and others to assist him in the ministry. Benny Moore later became Bishop Benjamin Moore. Eventually, Bishop Lewis moved to Santa Ana, California to start a ministry. After starting a church in Santa Ana, he moved to Florida. He found the climate in the State of Florida to be unbearable, so he relocated to the State of California. When he returned to California (Santa Cruz) from Florida, he brought Elder Robert Theobold and established him as pastor in Santa Cruz. After being the bishop of the Pacific Northwest for a period of time, Bishop Arthur Lewis began to experience health challenges again. He was placed on the P.A.W. directory of leaders as an honorary bishop. After a long period of battle, his health improved and he was once again reinstated to a full-fledged bishop; however, there were no vacant dioceses at the time. He was considered for the State of Ohio, but Bishop Karl Smith received the acknowledgment instead. This was the history of Bishop Lewis, one of the finest men we've ever had, but a man who was greatly afflicted over a number of years, and finally passed on to be with the Lord in 1973.

In 1929, there were four men elevated to the office of a bishop: R.G. Pettis, Samuel N. Hancock, Floyd I. Douglas, and Karl F. Smith. Bishop Samuel N. Hancock of Detroit, Michigan. He served the P.A.W. until 1931. In 1931, he was one of the leaders who consummated the merger of the Pentecostal Assemblies of Jesus Christ. In 1936, he found out about the racial platform of the Pentecostal Assemblies of Jesus Christ, but he still tried to go along with them and tried to help assist the organization for two additional years but to no avail. I left the PAJC that year. In 1938 Bishop Hancock finally gave up and returned to the Pentecostal Assemblies of the World and was reinstated as a bishop. He served as Diocesan Bishop over the State of Illinois until the year 1967. He and Bishop Willie Lee of Indianapolis left the Pentecostal Assemblies of the World and set up their own organization, the Pentecostal Churches of Apostolic Faith in 1967. In 1931, R.G. Pettis transitioned to the Pentecostal Assemblies of Jesus Christ and later, he was unfortunately dismissed from the organization due to some misconduct. Floyd I. Douglas served the P.A.W. as a bishop until his passing in 1951. Karl F. Smith served likewise until 1931, and in that year when the Pentecostal Assemblies of Jesus Christ was founded, he was one of the leaders of the movement. In 1938, he returned to the Pentecostal Assemblies of the World, and in 1940 he was reinstated to the office of bishop and served until his passing in 1972. I had the privilege of eulogizing him.

In 1932, one man was elevated to the office of a bishop and this was shortly after the death of Bishop G.T. Haywood and the one-year moratorium on the office of Presiding Bishop. Samuel Grimes was elevated to the office of a bishop, and eventually succeeded Bishop Haywood as the second Presiding Bishop of the P.A.W., a post he held until his death in 1967.

In 1934, there were two men elevated to the office of a bishop: Harry Barnett and Elmer F. Akers. Bishop Harry Barnett was a converted Jew of the tribe of Benjamin. He helped the organization greatly understand Jewish customs and history. I received knowledge from Bishop Harry Barnett that I would never have known in any other way. Our relationship was so close that the last six years in which he lived he was unable to carry out his work as a bishop; he only lived 60 miles from me in Kalamazoo. Any time he had a problem arise he would call me and I would go get him in my car and take him to his destination. On the way, he'd tell me what he wanted to be done and I would preside for him. Essentially, I was a bishop in training under Bishop Harry Barnett. I served six years in that capacity and then when Bishop Sypes was assigned over the State of Michigan for

11 years I served in the same capacity for him and so I had 17 years of on-the-job training before I was assigned to the State of Michigan. I was blessed and had advantages that no other person in the Pentecostal Assemblies of the World had. Bishop Barnett died in 1952.

Elmer F. Akers was located in Dayton, Ohio, and served until the year 1936 when he was dismissed from the position. He was succeeded by Bishop Ralph Bass. A man in a high position can fall and that's the reason Paul said, *Brethren, if any man be overtaken in a fault, ye which are spiritual, restore such a one in the spirit of meekness, fearing, less ye yourself also be tempted* (Galatians 6:1). What do I take away from that? Any person can be overtaken in a fault. I just want you to know, if you have heard the doctrine of Eternal Security that there is no truth in it. He has provided for our eternal security, but we have to make our calling and election sure.

In 1935 there were four men elevated to the office of a bishop: Benny H. Nelson, David Schultz, William Martin, and Fred L. Clark. Bishop Benny H. Nelson of Red Wing, Minnesota served from 1935 to 1947. Bishop Nelson was a construction contractor and he so involved in his construction business that he neglected the responsibilities of his diocese. The diocese brought an accusation of neglect against him. As Bishop Grimes expressed, it was not "malfeasance of office" but rather "nonfeasance of office." Hence, Bishop Nelson was retired to the status of an honorary bishop in 1947. Essentially, he left the P.A.W. due to that forced retirement. In 1961, he relinquished his contracting business and he returned to the Pentecostal Assemblies of the World and was reinstated as an honorary bishop until his death in 1971. Bishop David T. Schulz of Louisville, Kentucky was elevated to the office of a Bishop and he succeeded Floyd I. Douglas as pastor of Bethel Temple Church in Louisville, Kentucky when Bishop Douglas migrated to California. Bishop Schulz took over that church and served until his passing in 1972. It was my responsibility and privilege to eulogize him. The third bishop was Fred L. Clark of Warren, Ohio. He served the P.A.W. until his death in 1933. The final pastor elevated to the office of bishop in 1935 was William Martin of Dayton, Ohio. He served one year, and then he had to be dismissed and never returned to the Pentecostal Assemblies of the World.

In 1940, there were two men elevated to the office of a bishop: J.A. Rayl and Karl F. Smith. Bishop J.A. Rayl served for two years and then left the Pentecostal Assemblies of the World. He returned to the Pentecostal Assemblies of the World in 1957, but he served in an honorary bishop capacity for three years until his death. Bishop Karl F. Smith of Columbus, Ohio was installed as a bishop in the P.A.W. a second time because of his prior departure to the Pentecostal Assemblies of Jesus Christ. After his second elevation to the office of a bishop he served until his death in 1972. It was my responsibility and privilege to preach his funeral.

I'd like to tell you a little bit about Bishop Smith. He was saved and raised under Bishop R.C. Lawson and for that reason; he never had the contact with Bishop Haywood's ministry as many others had, so he knew nothing of it. Consequently, there were some differences in doctrinal points along the way, but nothing of any importance, so we felt perfectly free to have him as one of our bishops. I believe in his day he had the soundest mind of any man on the Board. After I was elected in the office of presiding bishop whenever I needed council it was Bishop Karl Smith that I went to. In his last years, he was often bedfast. He told me the following: "when I get up in the morning if I can get my shoes on, I can go to church tonight. If I can't get my shoes on, I've got to wait for another day." I went on more than one occasion to his bedroom and sat by his bed and asked his advice. My office outranked his, but that was the confidence that I had in him.

I'm not trying to say that one man is above another, but God gives every man special abilities and as we have had to go along with the Pentecostal Assemblies of the World and serve in the capacities I've had to serve, I had to know who had what, so that I could go to them. I'm not trying to be little somebody else; I just want you to know some of these high points in the lives of some of our bishops.

When Bishop Samuel Grimes died, I was elected into the office of presiding bishop for the remaining one-year term and after that term, there was an election. The voting activities transpired in Bishop Frank Reuben Bowdan's Home Assembly Church in Los Angeles, California in 1968 and I was re-elected with an overwhelming vote as the presiding bishop. On the last day of the convention after I offered the prayer of dismissal, Bishop Karl Smith stepped up behind me, took hold of my arm, and said, "Bishop Paddock, I want you to sit down. I want to talk to you before you mingle with the crowd or I won't have any other chance. "

We sat near each other and he said, "now, Bishop Paddock, I want you to know, we are most happy to have you as our presiding bishop, and we are so glad that there was no racism injected in the election. But Bishop, maybe you don't know us as well as you ought to. I'm going to tell you in advance, we are going to make you cry." I replied, "well, Bishop Smith, if I have to cry, then I have to cry. But I'm going to tell you in advance, it takes some doing to make me cry." The first time I ever came near crying was when I stood in his pulpit and over his casket before I eulogized him.

Over the years, the Pentecostal Assemblies of the World eventually made me cry. I recall, it was in Los Angeles, California in the Biltmore Hotel. There was a testimonial dinner for Bishop Bowdan and me. After Pastor Byron Brazier (he wasn't bishop then) made a wonderful speech that day, Bishop Robert McMurray stepped up to the podium and said, "now, we're going to have some remarks from both Bishop Paddock and Bishop Bowdan, but we can't have them now, because neither one of them can say a word." He was right because we both cried not for any racially charged behavior, but because of the overwhelming love that was shown to us.

In 1944, one man was elevated to the office of a bishop, James Leo Sipes. He was assigned to the Midwestern District Council, but after the death of Bishop Barnett, Bishop Sipes was transferred to the State of Michigan, the Northern District Council. He served as my bishop for 11 years and served in the P.A.W. until his death in 1962. It was my privilege to perform the eulogy at his funeral.

In 1949, two individuals were elevated to the office of a bishop: Oscar Sanders and S. R. Burrows. Bishop Sanders of Muncie, Indiana served until his death in 1973. I was honored and privileged to preach at his funeral (in each of the cases where I preached at these funerals, I had to take the responsibility of the church until arrangements could be made for them). Bishop S. R. Burrows served the organization for three years until he died. He was from Bedford, Kentucky. He had a small church, but he was a godly man. An example of his godliness, when his wife died 20 years before his role to the office of a bishop he stayed single for the rest of his life. He didn't play around and he didn't look for another wife. He was not well known around the organization. In fact, when he died Bishop Schulz, Bishop Sypes, and I was the only members of the Pentecostal Assemblies of the World leadership to attend his funeral. The family requested the service of a former preacher that was dismissed from the P.A.W. to eulogize him. This was one of the saddest things I've known of in my experience in the bishopric-he did not have the type of funeral that was appropriate for a bishop in the organization.

In 1950, there were two individuals elected to the office of a bishop during the convention in Boston, Massachusetts: Austin Lane and Freeman Thomas. Bishop Lane of St. Louis, Missouri served until he passed in 1967. I had the responsibility of preaching at the funeral. Bishop Freeman Thomas of Pittsburgh, Pennsylvania was the only bishop on the Executive Board that had seniority over me in the office of bishop. I was on the board for three years as a general treasurer and helped with his on boarding process when he was elected to the Executive Board of the P.A.W. Bishop Thomas was still an active bishop during the writing of this book.

In 1952, there was a pair of twins brought to the board (at least that's what they always called themselves). These individuals were me, Ross P. Paddock and John Caldwell. Bishop Caldwell and I had a brotherly relationship. I remember on instance during the latter part of Bishop Caldwell's life, I was with Bishop Willie Smith in Los Angeles, when one night they transported Bishop Caldwell from San Diego to Los Angeles to see me. He was unable to stand, so they seated on the pulpit and give him a microphone to share his testimony. As he testified, Bishop Caldwell said, "when I heard that Bishop Paddock was in California, I had to come and see my twin brother one more time before I died." While I was assigned to the Mountain States Council, he seldom missed those council meetings. He was a big supporter of my work and we worked together as he chaired that council for so many years. We loved one another so much.

In 1953, there were four men elevated to the office of a bishop: John S. Holly, Herbert Davis, Raymond Robinson, and Nobel Pace. Bishop Holly of Chicago, Illinois served in the P.A.W. until 1979 when he passed. Bishop Herbert Davis of Leavenworth, Kansas served until his passing in 1959. Raymond Robinson served as a bishop in the organization until 1966. Unfortunately, he was disqualified. Bishop Nobel Pace served in the P.A.W. for 10 years as a bishop and he passed in 1967. It was my responsibility and privilege to preach at his funeral.

In 1959, William Crossly was the sole person elevated to the office of bishop. He was a member of the Northern District Council for 30 years and served as its treasurer for 26 years. He was elected to the diocese of the Pacific Northwest District Council and Alaska, where he served for 3 years. Later, he organized and served the Western New York and Ontario Council for 15 years and eventually, his diocese expanded to include the entire State of New York and Eastern Canada. He held that role until his departure from this life.

In 1960, Ralph Bass was elected to the office of bishop and he served until his demise in June 1972. He was assigned to the State of Arkansas. It was my responsibility and privilege to preach at his funeral as well.

In 1962, three men were elevated to the office of a bishop: Lawrence Edwin Brisbin, Frank Reuben Bowdan, and Benjamin Moore. Bishop Brisbin of Grand Rapids, Michigan served until his passing on April 14, 1994, and Bishop Bowdan served until his demise in 1977. There are so many memories between Bishop Bowden and I. I remember being in a meeting with Elder Henry Johnson when I was informed about the death of my friend Bishop Bowdan. I was just returning from an out of town trip, and then I had to book a plane and fly for that funeral. I did not preach at the funeral, but I was there for almost 11 hours to pay my respects to the deceased and the family the night before the funeral. Bishop Bowdan and I had have been fellow laborers for quite some time. As a district elder and the secretary of the Northern District Council, when we attended councils, we lodged in the homes of fellow saints of those cities because of the lack of money for lodging accommodations. Typically, Elder Bowdan and I would share the same room and the same bed. As roommates, I found myself using my accountant experience to assist him in the council bookkeeping matters. The two of us would go to the room in the evenings and we'd work into the night getting the council financial records straightened out. In the morning, when my alarm rang, I'd let him go to the bathroom first and I'd stay and get a little extra sleep. Then when he'd come back to the room to finish dressing, I'd go to the bathroom. When I'd returned and look for my clothes, time after time I'd have to say, "Frank, give me my shirt so I can get dressed. He'd have some of my clothes on. Another instance, we went to New Haven, Connecticut to a mid-winter conference and I was supposed to preach that evening. After our meeting ended and I went to grab my hat and realized it was gone. It was a cold winter and I knew I couldn't go out of the building without a hat. Eventually, I bought another hat and the next morning Bishop Bowdan came to me and said, "Bishop Paddock, "I'm so sorry but I did it again." So, I went home with two hats. When he brought my hat back he said, "I put my hat on this morning, and my wife looked at me and said, 'Frank, that's not your hat.'" He said, "I took it off and looked at it and said, why it isn't even like my hat. So, I turned it over and looked in it and I saw your initials and said, Oh no, not again."

The third Bishop was the one I have always known as "Little Benny". I have known Bishop Benjamin Thomas Moore since he was just a little boy. Bishop Moore served the P.A.W. until he fell asleep in Christ in 1988.

In 1964, George Brooks was the only member of P.A.W. elevated to the office of bishop. Bishop George Brooks of New Haven, Connecticut was the oldest man on the Board of Bishops at the time of this manuscript. He is 84 years old and counting.

In 1965, three men were consecrated to the office of a bishop: Ramsey N. Butler of Washington, D.C., B.T. Jones of Princeton, West Virginia, and Clarence Allen of Hartford, Connecticut. Bishop Butler served until he passed away. Bishop B. T. Jones of Princeton, West Virginia led two councils. He was 79-years-old during the original publication of this manuscript and still active presiding over the West Virginia Council and the Virginia Council. Bishop Clarence Allen of Hartford, Connecticut passed in 1974 and I was unavailable to preach at his funeral because I was in surgery. Also, Bishop Hobart Taliaferro of Atlantic City, New Jersey and he served until he passed in 1968.

In 1966, one man, Elder Robert Walls of San Antonio, Texas, is still active today as the bishop over the Texas State Council.

In 1967, five men were elevated to the office of a bishop: Alfred Boyd, Archie Street, Thomas John Weeks, William Holder, and Clester Richard Lee. The first of the elevation was Bishop Alfred Boyd of Davenport, Iowa. He served the P.A.W. until his demise and the family called me to take the responsibility of preaching at his funeral in 1978. Bishop Archie Street served the organization until his death He was from Pine Bluff, Arkansas, and he presided over two dioceses: the Arkansas Council and the Louisiana State Council. Normally, as an organization, we will not take a diocese away from an individual presiding over multiple dioceses but when the person dies or becomes incapacitated, we will not allow the successor to preside over two dioceses as the predecessor.

Thomas Weeks of Boston, Massachusetts was elevated to the office of a diocesan bishop over the Caribbean Council of the P.A.W. In 1968, he was transferred from the Caribbean Council to the Massachusetts State Council as the diocesan bishop where he served over 41 years until he retired his diocesan bishop status. He is currently serving as an emeritus bishop.

Bishop William Holder of Marion, Indiana never had the opportunity to fully serve as diocesan bishop until he passed away in the mid-1980s. When he was elevated to the office of the diocesan bishop, he was unable to serve in the role due to his wife's health. He was confined at home to care for her until her death. After a period of mourning he regained some measure of strength and married again. It became my privilege to preach the 50th anniversary of his ministry and church in Marion, Indiana. We went over to visit the second wife who was at death's door at that time. We prayed for her but she was too far gone and soon after the Lord just took her home. Again, he was without a wife in his advanced age. Because of these catastrophic conditions, he never had the opportunity to serve on the board of bishops for the P.A.W.

Bishop C.R. Lee served the P.A.W. until he passed in his nineties in 1991. He was a diocesan bishop of the State of Ohio. Little known fact: Bishop Lee was the father-in-law of Bishop Benjamin Moore.

In 1968, there were four bishopric elevations, Bishop Phillip Lee Scott, Bishop James A. Johnson, Bishop Thomas Streitferdt, and Bishop Earl Parchia. Bishop Phillip Scott of St. Louis, Missouri, pastored one of the largest churches in the Pentecostal Assemblies of the World. He oversaw the Midwestern District Council of the P.A.W. It was my privilege to dedicate his $1.5 million church in St. Louis before he passed.

When Bishop James A. Johnson was designated and elevated to the office of bishop and placed over the Kansas/Colorado diocese, I lost him as my secretary on the P.A.W. Executive Board. I must tell you that his mother was an excellent evangelist, and when he was hardly more than a toddler, his mother held a meeting for us and that's how I became acquainted with the family. When he grew up and was saved, I knew him as a saved man. When God called him to the ministry, I knew him then as a saved young minister, and I sort of adopted him as my son. Fact of the matter is, he and his wife had their honeymoon in my home. I made him go for a two-week service shortly after his marriage, which was in effect their honeymoon.

Bishop Thomas Streitferdt was elevated to serve over the State of New Jersey. He built a church in Harlem that is a showplace and to such an extent that so many people were coming and going to marvel at his facility. The church was attracting such traffic that he had to tell staff not to allow any other tourist into the facility. This caused a conflict because Bishop Robert McMurray arrived in the city and went to see the church, but they wouldn't let him in. Of course, Bishop Streitferdt would have granted access to Bishop McMurray had he known about his visit to his church. Streitferdt served as the editor of the P.A.W. *Christian Outlook Magazine* and regularly broadcasted both on the radio and television. I had the privilege to be on his broadcast. Also, he had a complete printing press, and he printed a lot of literature and distributed it all over the country. Bishop Streitferdt was very active. Eventually, he left the Pentecostal Assemblies of the World and started his own organization.

Bishop Earl Parchia, Sr. served as the chairman of the Foreign Missionary Department of the Pentecostal Assemblies of the World and when he was elevated to the office of a bishop, he vacated the position. At the printing of this book, he is still active as bishop over the State of Florida. Incidentally, I had to preside as bishop over the State of Florida at two different times. Likewise, in Georgia, and the Carolinas, along with many others. The bylaws of the Pentecostal of Assemblies, when the presiding bishop becomes incapacitated or dies, calls for the assistant presider to assume the role of the presider, and if a bishop of a diocese passes, then the presiding bishop has to take the responsibility of that diocese until a diocesan bishop can be appointed. For instance, when Presiding Bishop Grimes died, immediately, I had to take over the states of Massachusetts, New York, Virginia, North and South Carolina, Georgia, Florida, Alabama, Mississippi, Missouri, a portion of Tennessee, Colorado, Kansas, and Illinois, along with the entire foreign missionary department of the Pentecostal Assemblies of the Word. All along, I was already serving as the Diocesan Bishop over the State of Michigan.

In 1972, there were three men elevated to the office of a bishop: Frances Leonard Smith, Morris Ellis Golder, and James Tyson. Bishop Smith became the diocesan of the Southern Tri-State Council of Mississippi, Alabama, and West Tennessee. Ultimately, he ascended to the Office of Presiding Bishop of the Pentecostal Assemblies of the World in 1974.

The Pentecostal Assemblies of the World elevated Morris E. Golder to the bishopric and placed him as the diocesan over the 11th Episcopal District of Tennessee and Kentucky.

Bishop Tyson oversees the Tri-State Council of the Pentecostal Assemblies of the World and had held that position since Bishop Alfred L. Boyd's incapacitation and eventual death. The Tri-State Council consisted of the following states for numerous years: Iowa, Nebraska, and Wyoming. There were no churches in Wyoming, but since Bishop Tyson's leadership over the diocese, a number of churches were established in Cheyenne and Casper, and they are establishing a church in Laramie, Wyoming. During the compilation of this book, Bishop Tyson was serving as a bishop over the State of Indiana.

In 1973, Pastor Robert Wilson McMurray, who held the office of Chairman of the California State Council of the Pentecostal Assemblies of the World, was asked to serve as Diocesan Bishop of the 20th Episcopal Diocese of Oklahoma. Ultimately, he was transferred to serve as Diocesan Bishop of California and Nevada District Council in 1977 and he was laid to rest in 1995.

In 1974, there were four men elevated to the office of bishop: Charles Watkins, Roosevelt Renick, David Brazil, and W.L. Smith. Elder Watkins was elevated by the Pentecostal Assemblies of the World, first to District Elder, then to National Minister of Music, and later in 1974 to the bishopric where he presided over the 4th Episcopal District in the State of Indiana.

Bishop Roosevelt S. Rennick served in the office of Diocesan Bishop for two years before he died. Again, it was my responsibility and privilege to preach at his funeral.

Bishop David Brazil, who has passed away, presided over the State of Georgia. Then there's Bishop W. L. Smith of Los Angeles; though he is of advanced age, he is alive and active. Bishop Smith has since retired from his diocese which was the State of Oklahoma.

In 1975, one man by the name, Bishop A. C. Eddings was elevated and he presided over the Mountain States Council.

In 1976, there were two promotions to the office of a bishop: Paul A. Bowers and Arthur Brazier. Bishop Paul A. Bowers, who is alive and very active, is presiding over the Carolina Council, which comprises both North and South

Carolina. The church he pastors is located in Cincinnati, Ohio. He recently built a very beautiful church and asked me to come down and preach the opening message in that church. The inaugural service drew a motorcade from the old church to the new church and was informed that it was the largest motorcade that the city of Cincinnati had ever seen. It extended for miles and the church was packed. During the inaugural service, something happened to me that day, I don't know what. I didn't realize it but after it was all over, Bishop Bowers said, "Bishop Paddock, do you know what you did?" I said, "What do you mean?" He said, "you preached for one hour and 45 minutes and you didn't preach like you were an old man. I don't know what happened, but we didn't lose any of the congregations during the service."

Bishop Arthur Brazier succeeded Bishop Holly as bishop over the State of Illinois. He was alive and very active at the time of publication of this manuscript.

In 1977, William L. Burrel of the State of Michigan was elevated to the office of a bishop. For years I called him my district elder because when I became bishop over the State of Michigan, he was the first district elder I appointed. A handsome young man, I knew him before he was married. We worked together so well over the years. I had a rather interesting experience a year and a half ago. I was there for Bible classes, and on Sunday night, his wife Sister Burrel in her testimony said, "I have adopted Bishop Paddock as my father in the gospel." So, I went home and told the saints I feel quite secure now, because I've been born twice and I've been adopted twice.

~ 9 ~

PIONEERS OF 20TH CENTURY PENTECOST

20TH CENTURY PIONEERS

Francis John "Frank" Ewart and Glen A. Cook both from the State of California. They were the first people known to be baptized in the name of Jesus. There was an interesting phenomenon that transpired between them. Since there no one around whom had their strong conviction about baptism, these two decided and baptized each other.

As I draw near to the conclusion of this manuscript, I would like to give a brief summary of the Pentecostal crusade in North America. Charles E. Parham led a bible school in Topeka, Kansas in 1901, where the Holy Ghost is known to have originally fallen in the United States. Later, William J. Seymour pioneered the Holy Spirit crusade in California known as the Azusa Street Mission.

J. J. Frazee was the first general superintendent of the Pentecostal Assemblies of the World. Eudorus Neander Bell, Howard A. Goss, Arch P. Collins, Daniel Charles Owen Opperman, L. C. Hall (he wrote and published the old Jesus-only songbook from which comes many of our current hymns; it was first called the Songs of Jesus). Williams Emmanuel Booth-Clibborn, Andrew Harvey Argue, Frank Small, George B. Studd, Elmer K. Fisher, Robert J. Scott, and M. R. Catlin. The latter was the presiding officer of the Pentecostal Assemblies of Jesus Christ when I originally joined that organization and was ordained as an elder. Robert E. McAlister was a founding member of Pentecostal Assemblies of Canada. Harry Morris, George Augustus Chambers, H. G. Rogers (founding member of Assemblies of God), B. F. Lawrence, Harry VanRoon, and R. L. Blankenship, A. C. Baker (he was the pastor of a church in Oregon City, and when he died his son assumed the pastorate role). S. D. Burroughs, O. F. Farris, D. H. Height, Grover Curly, Louis Liebowitz (he was converted Jew), S. C. McLain, Ben Pemberton, John Sheepy, and L. B. Sly. I personally knew Sly as a member in our church. He was also part of the missionary in South America for 50 years.

Spencer Leslie Wise and W. E. Tidson are prominent members in the history of 20th century Pentecost. As Presiding Bishop of the Pentecostal Assemblies of the World, I commissioned Bishop Morris E. Golder to research historical information about the organization, some of which came from Elder Tidson. During his research, Bishop Golder would ask me for information I could not furnish, but I would direct him to Elder Tidson for those answers.

E. W. Doak served as the second superintendent of the Pentecostal Assemblies of the World and one of the charter members of the corporation. T.C. Davis, whom I knew years ago, amused me one day because he said, "If there's anybody around who knows anything about organizations, I knew, because I helped start every one of them." It made me kind of wonder why he didn't stay with one of them. Robert C. Lawson, P.J.F. Bridges, and E. G. Lowe were other pioneers. Reverend Lowe was one of the individuals who received the Holy Ghost during the Azusa Street Mission. He preached for me on many occasions in Kalamazoo, Michigan. I gathered much historical information from him for this manuscript. George Carlisle was another historian who received the Holy Ghost in 1906 during the Azusa Street Mission. He preached for me a number of times and I gleaned much information from him as well.

Dunlap Chenault was the founder of the Pentecostal Apostolic work throughout the State of Texas. Guy Jamison, C.B. Gordon, O.D. Sheriff, C.R. Wilkes, R. Ragget, and James A. Thrush were other notable persons. Brother Thrush served as secretary of the Pentecostal Assemblies of Jesus Christ for a period. Earl D. Hill, Fred E. Pool, James Chin, and Andrew D. Urshan were others prominent figures. I knew the entire Urshan family; he was the father of Nathan Urshan, who at the time of the development of this Book was serving as the general superintendent of the United Pentecostal Churches.

George Washington, S.E. Cheeseman, B.L. Fitzpatrick, C.W. Phillio, L. V. Roberts, C.O. Waltman, A.N. Graves, J.D. Grover, R.A. Johnson, J.L. Kilbourne, and C.F. Longstreet. S.L. Ross, H.E. White, and William A. Mulford were other notable figures in the Pentecostal Apostolic movement. Elder Mulford preached the Easter morning message at Bishop Rowe's church in Mishawaka, Indiana, four months after I was baptized and filled with the Holy Ghost. I was a young minister at that time, and I was in that service from 5 a.m. until 11 at night. William Mulford was secretary of the Pentecostal Assemblies of Jesus Christ during that period, F. M. Lacey, A. Silverstein, and Oliver F. Foss (who served as one of the ordination committee members when I became an ordained minister in 1936).

J.W. Ledbetter was another prominent person in the Pentecostal movement. I knew him personally. He and his wife were part of P.A.W. missionaries in Africa. Life was very lean for them in Africa. There were times they did not have any meat for many days and they wanted meat so badly that one morning they got up to pray, and they asked God to give them some meat. After they prayed, he felt impressed to go hunting. Elder Ledbetter went to the woods and the Lord spoke to him and said, "There is your meat." He looked up in the tree and there was a monkey and he didn't know what to do about this. But he had prayed and the Lord said that's your meat. He shot the monkey, brought it home and Sister Ledbetter said, "What is this?" He said, "That's our meat." She said, "No way." He said, "we prayed and the Lord told me this was our meat." She cooked the monkey and they ate it. The Apostle Paul said, *every creature of God is good for food and nothing is to be refused if taken with thanksgiving. For it is sanctified by the word of God in prayer* (1 Timothy 4:4). Now, he didn't say you'd like it, rather, it's good for food.

J.C. Brickey, Martin Fray, Andrew D. Murray, E.C. Cheatham, M.E. Mills (one of the closest friends I ever had in this world), and Robert F. Tobin (served as the General Secretary of the Pentecostal Assemblies of the World for many years). Frank Coats, W.T. Witherspoon, Oscar Vega, and S.W. Chambers are notable figures. Brother Chambers was formerly the General Superintendent of the United Pentecostal Church. He did not acknowledge Bishop Brisbin and me when we sat in the front row of a past UPC convention. He knew we were present because one of the brethren of the UPC introduced us to him, but he still did not acknowledge our presence. On the contrary, when Brother Chambers attended the P.A.W. convention held in St. Louis during my tenure as the Presiding Bishop he was treated differently. Brother Chambers visited one of the main services one evening; I had him ushered right to the pulpit. I had our secretary pin an honorary bishop's badge on him and I immediately presented him to the congregation, and he made remarks. Afterward, he sat in a seat right next to me on the main stage. The next evening, he returned and I did the same thing. Someone asked me, "How could you do that for him?" I said, "Someone has to show him what it means to be saved."

William Stairs, Paul Box, S.G. Norris, A.T. Morgan, Smallwood Williams, Monroe Saunders, and A.D. VanHoos were other important members of the Pentecostal history. Reverend VanHoos was very active in the Pentecostal movement. He wrote a book about the 50 years of Pentecost and he has contacted me for information to use in his book.

These are the names of the men who have greatly contributed over the decades to the Pentecostal Assemblies of the World and to Pentecostalism in the 20th century. It would not be expedient to iterate all the accomplishment of each of these men.

What I have been discussing in this manuscript is the latter rain day, and not the early church that you read about in your Bible. You have the history of the Acts of the Apostles, the twenty-one Epistles, the four Gospels, and the Revelation of Jesus Christ. But that doesn't give you history of our church today. You may know some prophecies but what we are dealing with is history of the current Pentecostal church age. It's nice to know where we came from but it is far more important for us to know where we're going. It'll help us to get where we're going by knowing where we came from.

I was born 72 years ago to my mother and father. I also have a brother and a sister. But, when I was 21-years-old, I died. They took me and buried me in a watery grave in the name of Jesus Christ for the remission of my sins, and God filled me with the Holy Ghost. Subsequently, I was born again into a new family. The Scripture says that *if you forsake father, mother, sister and brother you will have fathers, mothers, sisters, brothers, houses and land a hundredfold and in the world to come, eternal life* (Matthew 19:21). For years, I have traveled around the U.S. and I found just that kind of family. But it's most difficult for me to find any fathers and mothers anymore at my current age because those that would be fathers and mothers to me in the faith have departed this life. Do you know what it makes me know? I must be one of the fathers, now.

The Pentecostal Assemblies of the World would be the largest denomination in the world today if there had never been any division. We would have overtaken this world. Unfortunately, we have been divided and separated, and our powers had been divided until the government of the United States recognized us only as a sect. It's unfortunate, and a shame. We would like to have the Pentecostal Assemblies of the World participate in a census data along with all the other members of the 46 organizations that are in the Apostolic World Christian Fellowship and show Washington, D.C. what the Jesus-only people have in this country. They will find out we're not the tail, but we are the head.

~ 10 ~

GREAT WOMEN OF
PENTECOST

WOMEN OF PENTECOST

As I draw near to the conclusion of this manuscript, it's important for me to mention some of the women that have made countless contributions to the Pentecostal movement around the world. Clearly, I've mentioned many men throughout this manuscript, but the book will be incomplete if I did not mention some of the women that impacted the history of Pentecost, including the women who stood with the men mentioned throughout this manuscript.

I was invited to Bishop Ralph Bass's church in Dayton, Ohio some years ago during one of the church pastoral anniversaries and the members of his church had both Bishop Bass and First Lady Bass nicely adorned for the occasion. The members offered very pleasant words and complemented the pastor and his wife. I heard so many nice compliments that Sunday morning from the saints about the Pastor and First Lady. But those who remember Bishop and Sister Bass knew he wasn't who you would refer to as a tall, dark, and handsome person. He was short and not too well shaped and Sister Bass was quite a large woman. When I got up to preach I turned around and took one last look and I said, "I want to say something that none of you have said. Just take a look at Bishop and Sister Bass, that's the perfection of beauty when God gets in you and shines.

A few years back in the days of the mini-skirt, I commonly said this in many churches: You don't have to show me you're a woman. I know you are. Just show me you're a lady.

In the beginning, when God looked at man and said it's not good for the man to be alone. I can tell you this, without women in this world, men would become slovenly beasts in a short time. We wouldn't care about grooming, we wouldn't care whether our faces were clean or dirty, and we wouldn't even bother to shave. Personally, I believe as the Bible said, it is a shame for a man to have long hair and for a woman to have her head covered. Paul in 1 Corinthians 11 was saying that wives should be under submission to their husband, and if they were not under submission, then they should be shorn because the hair was a badge or outward evidence that they were in submission to their husbands. Maybe you've never heard of this before but that's the way it was and your hair is given to you as a covering but your husband is the one that covers you or rules over you.

God recognized that it was not good for man to be alone and said, *I will make a helpmeet for him* (Genesis 2:18).I remember preaching at a funeral for a pastor's wife once and I took that statement as the text, and the people looked at me in amazement, but my subject was, "this man had a help-mate" (I personally knew the pastor and wife very well and knew the wife had been a real helpmate to him). I have heard behind every great man there's a great woman. I don't believe that, but behind great men are great women, and some great men are great in spite of their wives. We may as well recognize the truth, God said, *It is not good for the man to be alone* (Genesis 2:18). So, you say, "well He didn't say it wasn't good for the woman to be alone." Oh! Yes, He did. In the Book of 1 Corinthians chapter 11*Nevertheless neither is the man without the woman, neither the woman without the man, in the Lord* (1 Corinthians 11:11), because this is the way God ordained it. In my opinion, the church is incomplete without women. In reality, without women, there would not be a church.

God told the prophet to call together the weeping women, the praying women (Ezra 8:14). Why He didn't say, the weeping and praying men? Well, it wasn't that men didn't weep. If you recall, Jeremiah said that his tears would run down always. Sure, there are some men who weep, but call a church prayer meeting and find out who gets there. Generally, women were essential in the local church. Historically, if I was to go back to the beginning of the Pentecostal church movement, who was the first one in Elder Parham's school to receive the Holy Ghost? A woman, Agnes Ozman

There have been numerous women who have made great contributions to the Pentecostal movement over the years. One of those great women was Mattie Crawford. She was used by God tremendously in healing as well as preaching baptism in the name of Jesus. She preached with such an anointing that everywhere she served she left an impact for the Lord. For instance, Sister Crawford went into the City of South Bend where she preached a very successful meeting and as a result established what is the nucleus of the church that is today, a $1.5 Million church facility? Recently, the congregation just started another project that will be more than$2 million, pastorate by Bishop Worthy Rowe. Bishop Rowe is the son of the late Bishop G. B. Rowe (one of the bishops of the P.A.W.). Bishop Worthy Rowe is the Chairman of the Apostolic World Christian Fellowship and I serve as his vice-chairman.

Sister Crawford visited South Bend and did a great work. Unfortunately, later she turned away from the faith. The last news heard, she believed her power and gifts came from the stars. She became an astrologist.

There are numerous other women of the Pentecostal movement that come to mind: Mother Barkley in Africa, Mother Ledbetter, Mother McCarthy of India, Mother Mae Irie of China, and Sister Elizabeth Stieglitz of China.

Personally, I knew Sister Mae Irie. She has been in my church and residence. She was used mightily in China during World War II when Japan invaded China. During such time all Americans were asked to exit the country but Sister Stiglitz refused to leave the new converts. In short, this is my family and I'm not going to leave them. The Japanese put her in a concentration camp and mistreated her to the extent that she completely lost her sanity after which they sent her back home to the United Sates. She lives with her daughter in Benton Harbor, Michigan which is 50 miles from my hometown Kalamazoo. Sister Stiglitz's mental illness was so severe that her daughter was incapable of caring for her and relinquished to the County health department in Kalamazoo. When I learned of it, I told her daughter I will certainly go up and visit her. She said, "no, don't go. She wouldn't know you and you would only aggravate her." So, she said, "don't go, just pray." She died after having served the Pentecostal Assemblies of the World for so many years. Another organization oversaw her funeral. It so happened that I was close enough there that I read it in a local paper, and having another one of our bishops holding a meeting for me at that time, we went over to the funeral and represented the Pentecostal Assemblies of the World.

Another notable evangelist is Ellen Moore Hopkins. She was a foreign evangelist, a native African who came to the U.S. and was educated and returned to Africa under the P.A.W. banner as a missionary. She has done a very great work. We have had only one woman in any top office in the Pentecostal Assemblies of the World and that was one of the pastors in my diocese, Pastor Lottie Glenn, who served for six years as a lay director with equal legislative rights with the bishops.

In 1946, the P.A.W. convention was hosted by Diocesan Bishop Douglas in Los Angeles, California. There was a sister (I believe her name was Marion Williams) from Edna, New Jersey. She taught a bible survey in the P.A.W. national convention. When I was the Presiding Bishop, I chose Pastor Lottie Glenn to teach the Bible class, and when we arrived, Pastor Glenn's husband had become quite ill and she could not come to the convention. So, I substituted her with Sister Letha Collins of Leavenworth Kansas, and she did a remarkable job.

There have been women who have done great things in the Pentecostal Assemblies of the World. The P.A.W. women auxiliary or missionary department has done great things. To name other great women, Pastor/Sister Clark of Ohio, Sister Lulu Jackson of Michigan, and the list goes on. In the P.A.W. Sunday School Department and Home Missionary Department as well as various auxiliaries, countless women have done great work. We have had some very godly women, some of the greatest women who have ever walked on this earth. Praise the Lord! Many of them, I've been happy to call Mother and all of them, I'm happy to just call "sister". The sisters were wonderful and the P.A.W. could not do without them. The reasons women were not mentioned as much throughout this manuscript is because of what I was tasked to deal with during this writing. When Jesus comes for the church, He is returning for that which is called the "Body of Christ." My prayer for you is that you know this Jesus when He comes for His people. You must be born again of the water and spirit in accordance with the Book of Acts 2:4.

AUTHOR'S BIOGRAPHY

Bishop Ross Perry Paddock became a member of the Pentecostal Assemblies of the World Executive Board in 1947. During the development of the original manuscript, he was the oldest member of the P.A.W. Executive Board. From 1947 until 1978, every member is now deceased; hence, it made him the oldest member of the Board. He was directly connected to the election of all the current members (1978) on the Board. Also, during the development of this book, there was only one bishop who was senior to him in the bishopric, and that was Bishop Freeman Thomas of Pittsburgh, Pennsylvania. However, Paddock was on the Executive Board for three years before Thomas was elected to the board as treasurer. It was two years after Thomas became a bishop, that Paddock was elevated to the office of bishop. Bishop Paddock was second in the bishopric seniority; however, he was the senior member of the Executive Board in terms of tenure on the Executive Board. The following statements are in Bishop Paddock's words: "I have considered the words of David: he said, *I have been young, and now am old; yet have I not seen the righteous forsaken, nor his seed begging bread* (Psalm 37:25). I was young and now I am old linger in my mind. The Scripture plainly emphasizes that David was *very* old when he penned his psalms. I am several years older than David was when those words were spoken of him. So, if he was *very* old, I guess that makes me pretty ancient. I remember reading Apostle Paul's words to Philemon and he used the expression, *I am such the one as Paul the aged.* I am about 16 years older than Paul was when he said that. Well, if he was an aged man at that age, then what am I now? Then I stop to think of some of my predecessors, two of the greatest men we had with us: the late Bishop Garfield T. Haywood and Elder Robert F. Tobin. Both of them preached themselves to death. Now, I have preached more years than either of them and I am several years older (almost 20) than they were at the time they died. When I think about those things, I feel pretty ancient at times. I read in the Scripture *that Jesus sat and taught the people.* If He did that when he was 32 years old, I guess it is all right for me to give you a little of my background to let you know that there is a reason for my knowledge of the things that I covered in this Book. I trust you will be blessed by these writings. Amen! Bishop Ross Perry Paddock, the great warrior for the kingdom of God, was called home, Monday, September 17, 1990.

NOTES

Barrett, D.B. (1988). The Twentieth-Century Pentecostal Charismatic Renewal in the Holy Spirit, with its Goal of World Evangelization. Retrieved from https://doi.org/10.1177/239693938801200303.

Bellitto, C.M. (2002). The General Councils: A History of the Twenty-One General Councils from Nicaea to Vatican II: A History of the Twenty-one Church Councils from Nicaea to Vatican II. New York, NY: Paulist Press.

Foxe, J. (2009). Fox's Book of Martyrs. Blacksburg, VA: Wilder Publications.

Frost, D., & Graham, B. (1997). Personal Thoughts of a Public Man. Colorado Springs, CO: Chariot Victor.

Geertz, C.(1973). Religion as a Cultural System.

Graham, H. (2000). Indigenous Religions: A Companion. New York, NY: Cassell

Melton, J.G. (2003). Encyclopedia of American Religions (Seventh edition). Farmington Hills, MI: The Gale Group, Inc.

Smith, C., &Prokopy, J. (1999). Latin American Religion in Motion. New York, NY: Routledge.

Stannus, H.H. (2015). A History of the Origin of the Doctrine of the Trinity in the Christian Church. Palala Press.

Steinmetz, D.C. (2001). Reformers in the Wings: From Geiler Von Kaysersberg to Theodore Beza. Oxford, UK: Oxford University Press.

Synan, V. (2001). In the Latter Days: The Outpouring of the Holy Spirit in the Twentieth Century. New York, NY: Xulon Press.

Talal Asad, T. (1982). The Construction of Religion as an Anthropological Category.

Thomas, W.H.(2016). The Apostle John: Studies in His Life and Writings.New York, NY: Crossreach Publications.

Tyson, J. L. (1992). The Early Pentecostal Revival: History of the Twentieth-Century Pentecostals and the Pentecostal Assemblies of the World, 1901-30.

Vergote, A. (1997). Religion, belief and unbelief: a psychological study, Leuven University Press.

OTHER BOOKS BY R. P. PADDOCK

➢ *The Seven Stages of the Resurrection*
➢ *The Unscripturalness of Unconditional Eternal Se-*
   curity
➢   *Restoration*
➢ *The Church an Organized Body*
➢ *Marriage and Divorce*
➢ *Apostolic Gleanings*
➢ *God's Financial Plan for the Church*
➢ *God's Standard of Dress for our Day*
➢ *Put Thee in Remembrance*
➢ A Narrative History of Bishop Garfield T. Haywood

BOOKS ON THE HISTORY OF PENTECOST

Bartleman, F. (1928). How Pentecost Came to Los Angeles. (Republished as Another Wave Rolls In, edited by John Walker and John G. Myers, Voce Publications, Box 672 Northridge, California, 91324).

Carl Brumback, C. (1961). Suddenly from Heaven. Gospel Publishing House: Springfield, MO (this Book has been reprinted as A Sound from Heaven and Like as a River in 1977).

Conn, C.W. (1955). Like A Mighty Army. Church of God Publishing House: Cleveland, TN.

Flower, A.R. (1962). Grace for Grace. Springfield, MO.

Frodsham, S. H. (1926). With Signs Following. Gospel Publishing House: Springfield, Missouri. Harper, M. (1965). As at The Beginning, by, Logos International, Plainfield, N.J.

Gee, D. (1941). The Pentecostal Movement. Victory Press: Clapham Crescent, London. Warner, W.E. (1978). Touched by the Fire. Logo International: Plainfield, N.J.

Herman, H.L. (2017). Fundamentals ofPentecostal Oneness. Alpha Omega Publishing Company: Jackson, MI.

Klaud, K.E. (1961). The Promise Fulfilled. Gospel Publishing House: Springfield, MO.

Lawrence, B.F. (1916). The Apostolic Faith Restored. Gospel Publishing House: Springfield, Missouri. (Now out of print.)

Menzies, W.W. (1971). Anointed to Serve. Gospel Publishing House: Springfield, Missouri, 1971.

Myland, D.W. (1910). The Latter Rain Covenant. The Evangel Publishing House: Chicago, IL. (Reprinted by A. N. Trotter, P.O. Box 26, Billings, MO. 65610).

Nichol, J.T. (1966).The Pentecostals. Logos International: Plainfield, N.J.

Nickel, T.R. (1962). In Those Days. Whitaker Brooks: Monroeville, PA.

Shakarian, D. (1975). The Happiest People on Earth. Fleming H. Revell: Old Tappan, New Jersey.

Synan, V. (1971). The Holiness-Pentecostal Movement in the United States. W. B. Eerdmans Publishing Company: Grand Rapids, Michigan.

Warner, W.E. (1978). They Saw It Happened!. Logos International: Plainfield, N.J.

www.ingramcontent.com/pod-product-compliance
Lightning Source LLC
Chambersburg PA
CBHW030842090426
42737CB00009B/1070